FAMILY APPROACHES IN TREATMENT OF EATING DISORDERS

Clinical Practice

Number 15

Judith H. Gold, M.D., F.R.C.P.(C)
Series Editor

FAMILY APPROACHES IN TREATMENT OF EATING DISORDERS

Edited by

D. Blake Woodside, M.D., M.Sc., F.R.C.P.(C)

Staff Psychiatrist, Eating Disorder Centre, The Toronto Hospital;
Assistant Professor, Department of Psychiatry, University of
Toronto, Toronto, Canada

Lorie Shekter-Wolfson, M.S.W., C.S.W.

Corporate Manager, Department of Social Work, and Former
Director of Family Services, Eating Disorder Centre, The Toronto
Hospital; Field Practicum Professor, Department of Social Work,
and Lecturer, Department of Psychiatry, University of Toronto,
Toronto, Canada

Washington, DC
London, England

Note: The authors have worked to ensure that all information in this book concerning drug dosages, schedules, and routes of administration is accurate as of the time of publication and consistent with standards set by the U.S. Food and Drug Administration and the general medical community. As medical research and practice advance, however, therapeutic standards may change. For this reason and because human and mechanical errors sometimes occur, we recommend that readers follow the advice of a physician who is directly involved in their care or the care of a member of their family.

Books published by the American Psychiatric Press, Inc., represent the views and opinions of the individual authors and do not necessarily represent the policies and opinions of the Press or the American Psychiatric Association.

American Psychiatric Press, Inc.
1400 K Street, N.W., Washington, DC 20005

The paper used in this publication meets the minimum requirements of the American National Standard for Information Sciences—Permanence of Paper for Printed Library Materials, ANSI Z39.48-1984.   ∞

Library of Congress Cataloging-in-Publication Data

Family approaches in treatment of eating disorders / edited by D. Blake
   Woodside, Lorie Shekter-Wolfson. — 1st ed.
      p. cm. — (Clinical practice ; no. 15)
      Includes bibliographical references.
      Includes index.
      ISBN 0-88048-180-3
      1. Eating disorders—Treatment. 2. Family psychotherapy.
   I. Woodside, D. Blake, 1957–   . II. Shekter-Wolfson, Lorie, 1951-
   III. Series.
      [DNLM: 1. Anorexia Nervosa—therapy. 2. Bulimia—therapy. 3. Family Therapy. W1 CL767J no. 15 / WM 175 F1984]
   RC552.E18F37   1991
   616.85′26—dc20
   DNLM/DLC
   for Library of Congress   90-896
                                                                       CIP

British Library Cataloguing in Publication Data

A CIP record is available from the British Library.

Contents

Contributors

Jack S. Brandes, M.D., Ph.D., F.R.C.P.(C)
Director of Family Therapy Training, Toronto Western Hospital;
Assistant Professor, Department of Psychiatry, University of
Toronto, Toronto, Canada

Christopher Dare, M.D., M.R.C.P., D.P.M., F.R.C.Psych.
Consultant Psychiatrist, Department of Children and
Adolescents, Bethlehem Royal and Maudsley Hospital, Denmark
Hill; Senior Lecturer, Department of Psychiatry, Institute of
Psychiatry, University of London, London, England

Paul E. Garfinkel, M.D., F.R.C.P.(C)
Psychiatrist-in-Chief, The Toronto Hospital; Professor and Vice-
Chairman, Department of Psychiatry, University of Toronto,
Toronto, Canada

Sidney Kennedy, M.B., F.R.C.P.(C)
Director, Eating Disorder Services, The Toronto General
Hospital; Associate Professor, Department of Psychiatry,
University of Toronto, Toronto, Canada

Donna MacAulay, M.S.W., C.S.W.
Social Worker, Toronto, Canada

Laura Giat Roberto, Psy.D.
Director, Eating Disorder Program, Eastern Virginia Family
Therapy Institute, Virginia Beach, Virginia

Lorie Shekter-Wolfson, M.S.W., C.S.W.
Corporate Manager, Department of Social Work, and Former
Director of Family Services, Eating Disorder Centre, The
Toronto Hospital; Field Practicum Professor, Department of
Social Work, and Lecturer, Department of Psychiatry, University
of Toronto, Toronto, Canada

George Szmukler, M.D., D.P.M., F.R.C.Psych., F.R.A.N.Z.C.P.
Consultant Psychiatrist, Royal Melbourne Hospital; Senior Associate, Department of Psychiatry, University of Melbourne, Melbourne, Australia

D. Blake Woodside, M.D., M.Sc., F.R.C.P.(C)
Staff Psychiatrist, Eating Disorder Centre, The Toronto Hospital; Assistant Professor, Department of Psychiatry, University of Toronto, Toronto, Canada

Introduction
to the Clinical Practice Series

Over the years of its existence the series of monographs entitled *Clinical Insights* gradually became focused on providing current, factual, and theoretical material of interest to the clinician working outside of a hospital setting. To reflect this orientation, the name of the Series has been changed to *Clinical Practice.*

The Clinical Practice Series will provide readers with books that give the mental health clinician a practical clinical approach to a variety of psychiatric problems. These books will provide up-to-date literature reviews and emphasize the most recent treatment methods. Thus, the publications in the Series will interest clinicians working both in psychiatry and in the other mental health professions.

Each year a number of books will be published dealing with all aspects of clinical practice. In addition, from time to time when appropriate, the publications may be revised and updated. Thus, the Series will provide quick access to relevant and important areas of psychiatric practice. Some books in the Series will be authored by a person considered to be an expert in that particular area; others will be edited by such an expert who will also draw together other knowledgeable authors to produce a comprehensive overview of that topic.

Some of the books in the Clinical Practice Series will have their foundation in presentations at an annual meeting of the American Psychiatric Association. All will contain the most recently available information on the subjects discussed. Theoretical and scientific data will be applied to clinical situations, and case illustrations will be utilized in order to make the material even more relevant for the practitioner. Thus, the Clinical Practice Series should provide educational reading in a compact format especially written for the mental health clinician–psychiatrist.

Judith H. Gold, M.D., F.R.C.P.(C)
Series Editor
Clinical Practice Series

Clinical Practice Series Titles

Treating Chronically Mentally Ill Women (#1)
Edited by Leona L. Bachrach, Ph.D., and Carol C. Nadelson, M.D.

Divorce as a Developmental Process (#2)
Edited by Judith H. Gold, M.D., F.R.C.P.(C)

Family Violence: Emerging Issues of a National Crisis (#3)
Edited by Leah J. Dickstein, M.D., and Carol C. Nadelson, M.D.

Anxiety and Depressive Disorders in the Medical Patient (#4)
By Leonard R. Derogatis, Ph.D., and Thomas N. Wise, M.D.

Anxiety: New Findings for the Clinician (#5)
Edited by Peter Roy-Byrne, M.D.

The Neuroleptic Malignant Syndrome and Related Conditions (#6)
By Arthur Lazarus, M.D., Stephan C. Mann, M.D., and Stanley N. Caroff, M.D.

Juvenile Homicide (#7)
Edited by Elissa P. Benedek, M.D., and Dewey G. Cornell, Ph.D.

Measuring Mental Illness: Psychometric Assessment for Clinicians (#8)
Edited by Scott Wetzler, Ph.D.

Family Involvement in Treatment of the Frail Elderly (#9)
Edited by Marion Zucker Goldstein, M.D.

Psychiatric Care of Migrants: A Clinical Guide (#10)
By Joseph J. Westermeyer, M.D., M.P.H., Ph.D.

Office Treatment of Schizophrenia (#11)
Edited by Mary V. Seeman, M.D., F.R.C.P.(C), and Stanley E. Greben, M.D., F.R.C.P.(C)

The Psychosocial Impact of Job Loss (#12)
By Nick Kates, M.B.B.S., F.R.C.P.(C), Barrie S. Greiff, M.D., and Duane Q. Hagen, M.D.

New Perspectives on Narcissism (#13)
Edited by Eric M. Plakun, M.D.

Clinical Management of Gender Identity Disorders in Children and Adults (#14
Edited by Ray Blanchard, Ph.D., and Betty W. Steiner, M.B., F.R.C.P.(C)

Family Approaches in Treatment of Eating Disorders (#15)
Edited by D. Blake Woodside, M.D., M.Sc., F.R.C.P.(C), and Lorie Shekter-Wolfson, M.S.W., C.S.W.

Adolescent Psychotherapy (#16)
Edited by Marcia Slomowitz, M.D.

Benzodiazepines in Clinical Practice: Risks and Benefits (#17)
Edited by Peter P. Roy-Byrne, M.D., and Deborah S. Cowley, M.D.

Current Treatments of Obsessive-Compulsive Disorder (#18)
Edited by Joseph Zohar, M.D., and Michele Tortora Pato, M.D.

Foreword

*T*his book addresses the role of family interventions for people with the eating disorders anorexia nervosa and bulimia nervosa, in the light of recent developments in their understanding. During the past decade, a multidimensional risk-factor model conceptualizing these disorders has generally been accepted. Such a model describes an interplay of predisposing forces. For particular individuals with an illness, the exact interactions of predisposing factors will vary, but these are often combinations of phenomena within the individual, family, and culture. Such risk factors are generally quite different from factors that precipitate the disorder, and they may be quite different from circumstances that perpetuate the disorder. The sustaining factors in the eating disorders are extraordinarily varied and include the psychobiological changes that occur with starvation and repeated binge eating and purging, a deterioration in vocational and social skills, lowered self-worth, and changes in the family.

Because of the many factors involved in sustaining these disorders and in their pathogenesis, and because of the multiple complications that may develop—including significant psychiatric impairment and various metabolic sequelae—more and more clinicians have turned to treatment programs that integrate various treatment components according to a particular patient's needs. To some, such developments suggest a weakening of theoretical premises about the nature of eating disorders; but for most, these developments suggest a practical approach to treatment guided by a healthy pragmatism—the patient's perceived needs. Such multifaceted treatment programs, when sensitively applied to specific patients, are an excellent example of eclecticism at its best.

When such multifaceted treatments are prescribed for patients, the nature of the treatment of the family must be clearly considered in each situation. Family involvement in anorexia nervosa has been widely recognized since the time of Gull and Lasègue, and the nature of this involvement and how to intervene have been the subjects of considerable speculation.

Woodside and Shekter-Wolfson have carefully prepared this volume for practicing clinicians involved in treating patients with eating disorders in various settings. Patients are recognized to be heterogeneous in their requirements for treatment; this includes the nature of the family involvement as well. Indications for family therapy and pitfalls and problems in such therapies are discussed in detail. In addition, the specific tailoring of the family treatment for inpatient and day-hospital settings is covered, as well as engaging and treating these families in a solo outpatient setting. The role of a family relations group as an adjunct to or replacement for family treatment for adults is the subject of a separate chapter. Finally, the structure and function of family support groups are considered.

Future developments in this field require the results of controlled studies to determine the precise nature of specific familial changes and of optimal specific treatments, such as the Maudsley study described in Chapter 1. Until such information is available, this book will provide practitioners with a state-of-the-art practical approach to families of eating-disordered patients.

Paul E. Garfinkel, M.D., F.R.C.P.(C)

Introduction

*T*he role of the family therapist in the treatment of the eating disorders anorexia nervosa and bulimia nervosa has a long and complex history. As long as a century ago, Gull (1874) and Lasègue (1873) advocated separation of the patient from the family as an essential component of treatment. Interest in the family then waned for several decades, only to reemerge gradually as the psychoanalytic movement gained force in the middle of the 20th century. Although psychoanalytic theories of familial contributions are no longer generally accepted, observations of individuals such as those by Masterson (1965) and Bruch (1979) have provided valuable insights into the inner world of the eating-disordered patient and spurred further investigation into family process.

The 1970s saw the development of two parallel influences, both of great importance to family therapists involved in the treatment of eating-disordered patients. The first was the seminal work of the Milan and Philadelphia schools (Minuchin et al. 1978; Selvini-Palazzoli 1974), providing for the first time a firm theoretical grounding on which to understand anorexia nervosa from a truly systematic perspective. Since this time, other theorists (Roberto et al. 1988; Schwartz et al. 1985) have expanded on and extended these theories to provide a systematic understanding of bulimia nervosa.

The second critical development was an understanding of the multidetermined nature of these enormously complex illnesses and of the need for multidimensional treatment approaches (Garfinkel and Garner 1982). Such treatment approaches actually may bear some general relationship to systems theory, as they stress not only the complexity of the individual's psychological situation but also insist on an appreciation of the larger family and social context in which individuals suffering from anorexia nervosa and bulimia nervosa operate.

Within this framework, we believe that the family therapist has a critical and important role in providing a clearer picture of predisposing and initiating factors in eating disorders, and in proposing interventions to address family-related perpetuating factors. We also believe, however, that it will be a rare case of either illness that will be comprehensively treated by family therapy alone. With this in mind, we see family intervention as an essential component of any comprehensive treatment program for eating disorders.

The purpose of this volume is to describe, in various clinical settings, the role of the family therapist. Although some of the chapters deal with highly specialized treatment units, such as the day-hospital program (Chapter 5) or the inpatient unit (Chapters 2 and 7), we believe that many of the interventions described are applicable to outpatient treatment settings. Two chapters (3 and 4) deal with the special problems faced by the outpatient family therapist when dealing with this clinical group. We have included chapters on a novel group therapy approach to family issues (Chapter 6) and on family support groups (Chapter 8), primarily to aid the family therapist who is treating patients who are concurrently engaged in outpatient group therapy programs, although both could be valuable if family therapy was not feasible.

There is an assumption—whether implicit or explicit—built into most of the chapters in this book—that the family therapist is not working in total isolation, that he or she will be coordinating treatment strategies with other health care professionals. This is not an accident; it is the philosophy of all of the authors.

Finally, readers should note that therapeutic approaches for adolescents are somewhat different from those for adult patient groups. Chapters 2 and 7, each dealing with inpatient treatment programs, demonstrate clearly these differences. Clarifying what family interventions are most appropriate for older versus younger age groups is a question that urgently requires attention. In this light, the ground-breaking investigations by George Szmukler and Christopher Dare (Chapter 1) deserve careful attention by all practitioners in the field.

In summary, our hope is that this volume will send the message that an eclectic, multidimensional approach to the family in the management of eating disorders is most likely to produce clinical improvement. We believe that we are all engaged in a vital clinical area, and we look forward to more developments in the next decade.

Chapter 1

The Maudsley Hospital Study of Family Therapy in Anorexia Nervosa and Bulimia Nervosa

GEORGE SZMUKLER, M.D., D.P.M., F.R.C.Psych., F.R.A.N.Z.C.P.
CHRISTOPHER DARE, M.D., M.R.C.P., D.P.M., F.R.C.Psych.

Chapter 1

The Maudsley Hospital Study of Family Therapy in Anorexia Nervosa and Bulimia Nervosa

*T*he search for effective treatments for anorexia nervosa is of considerable importance, since there is strong evidence that the disorder is increasing in incidence and its outcome is often poor. The disorder, as seen by physicians, usually follows a prolonged course, commonly lasting more than 3 years even in cases with good outcomes. Studies reviewing outcome after 4–8 years indicate a mortality rate of 2–5% and chronic illness in 20–30% (Szmukler and Russell 1986).

In this chapter, we describe a controlled treatment trial of family therapy and contrast it with a form of supportive individual psychotherapy conducted at the Maudsley Hospital, which began in 1979 and for which follow-up evaluations are still in progress. Other results from this trial have been reported elsewhere (Russell et al. 1987). The results to date concern the outcome 1 year after the start of treatment. This study illustrates the feasibility of controlled clinical trials of family therapy and some of the major problems in their conduct and in interpretation of the results.

The design and stages of the study are summarized in Figure 1. Each patient was initially admitted, as an inpatient, to a unit specializing in the treatment of eating disorders and having a primary goal of weight restoration to an optimal level. With experienced and skilled nurses, this is usually readily achieved. Following a return to a near-optimal weight (a mean of 89.5% of standard table weight [percentage of average body weight] was reached in this study over an average of 10.4 weeks in the hospital), the second stage of treatment was initiated just before discharge from the hospital. Patients were randomly allocated to family therapy or individual therapy to be given on an outpatient basis for as long as 1 year after discharge. The relative effectiveness of these treatments was the subject of the study, and a third stage of the investigation involved a follow-up and assessment of outcome.

From the outset of the study, it was appreciated that the patient population would not be homogeneous. It was thought necessary to divide the patients into several groups on the basis of likely outcome predicted from known prognostic factors: age at onset, duration of illness, and the presence of bulimia nervosa concurrently with anorexia nervosa. A later age at onset, a longer duration of illness, and the presence of bulimia nervosa are thought to be associated with a poorer outcome. The four prognostic groups selected are shown in Figure 1. Group 1 is designated as early onset, short history; Group 2 is early onset, long history; Group 3 is late onset; and Group 4 is anorexia nervosa with bulimia nervosa. After allocation to the appropriate groups, patients were randomly allocated to one of the two treatments.

It was considered important to take some account of possible variations in the experience, skills, and enthusiasm of the therapists. This was achieved by adopting a design ensuring that each therapist conducted both treatments and each was allocated approximately equal numbers of patients for family and individual therapy. The therapists were independent of the inpatient treatment team and introduced themselves to a patient shortly before the patient's discharge from the hospital.

During the study, four therapists were responsible for treating most of the patients. They were nonmedical clinicians (three social workers and one psychologist) who had been trained in both individual therapy and family therapy in appropriate recognized institutes.

Both therapies were closely and equally supervised for 1 hour per week by highly experienced clinicians in the field—Christopher Dare for family therapy and Gerald Russell for individual therapy. Sessions re-

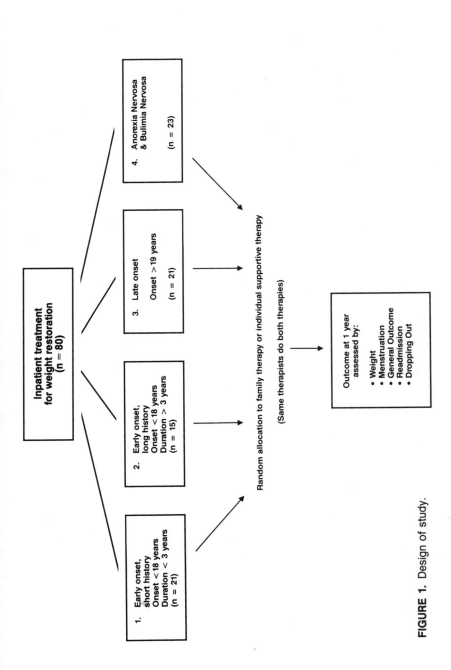

FIGURE 1. Design of study.

corded on videotape were frequently used in the supervision of both therapies, and the supervisory group included all of the therapists and the chief investigator, George Szmukler, who was not involved in treating families. During these sessions, special attention was paid to the possibility that therapists might show a greater enthusiasm for one treatment than for the other, which might confound results. It was the supervisor's clear impression, however, that the therapists worked especially hard regardless of the type of treatment.

Treatment sessions lasted 1 hour, and an attempt was made to match the frequency of the sessions for the two types of treatment. It was planned to treat the patients approximately fortnightly for the first 3 months and then reduce frequency to once every 3 weeks and then monthly. Some flexibility was required depending on the patients' clinical progress, practical constraints (such as distance of domicile from the hospital), and compliance.

Patients

Eighty consecutively admitted inpatients with a diagnosis of anorexia nervosa were included in the study. Primarily, they were a severely affected group with a low mean weight on admission (69.9% average body weight) and a long duration of illness (3.8 years). Forty-nine of the patients had at least one previous admission. The mean ages and duration of illness in the four prognostic groups are shown in Table 1.

Table 1. Patients' mean age and duration of illness

Prognostic group	Age		Duration of illness	
	Years	SD	Years	SD
Early onset, short history	16.6	1.7	1.2	0.7
Early onset, long history	20.6	4.0	5.9	2.0
Late onset	27.7	7.8	3.0	2.7
Anorexia nervosa and bulimia nervosa	24.0	8.4	4.9	3.7

Assessments

Clinical

At admission and during follow-up assessments, various measures examining clinical outcome were made, including body weight, the presence of menstruation, and a set of scales rating a patient's adjustment on five dimensions (Morgan and Russell 1975). These dimensions are nutritional status, menstrual function, mental state, psychosexual adjustment, and socioeconomic functioning. Scores are based on the 6-month period preceding the interview, and they may be combined to give average outcome measures.

Another major indicator of outcome was the need for readmission to the hospital after a relapse.

Family

The major family assessment measure used was parental expressed emotion (EE) as developed by workers at the Medical Research Council (MRC) Social Psychiatry Unit at the Institute of Psychiatry in London. This measure of relatives' attitudes to a patient is based on a semistructured interview with a single relative, which is recorded on audiotape. The interview lasts about 1 hour and is mainly concerned with eliciting a relative's account of the patient's problems and behavior and the reaction to them. The EE measure is of proven reliability and validity, as has been demonstrated in numerous studies. Special training is required to rate the component scales reliably. Expressed emotion has been demonstrated as an excellent predictor of relapse in patients with schizophrenia and probably in patients with depression (Leff and Vaughn 1980).

Five scales are rated from a replay of the audiotape: 1) critical comments made about the patient (a simple count); 2) hostility to the patient (0–3); 3) emotional overinvolvement, based on expressions by a relative of overconcern, overprotectiveness, and exaggerated emotional responses to the patient's illness (0–5); 4) warmth of feeling toward the patient (0–5); and 5) positive comments about the patient (a simple count). In all of these ratings, the tone of voice and the content of the comments are important to the assessment. Leff and Vaughn (1985) described the details of these procedures.

Despite the proven empirical usefulness of EE, the precise nature of what it measures, in terms of family interactions, is unknown.

The interview in this study was carried out soon after the patient's admission to the hospital. It was not possible to derive EE ratings during follow-up assessments.

Therapies

The family therapy is described in detail in Chapter 2. The individual therapy was intended to emulate the customary follow-up care of patients treated in the eating disorders unit. But the treatment trial for the individual therapy was more systematic, more frequent, and more closely supervised, and it had longer sessions than usual. The therapy was supportive, educational, and problem centered, with elements of cognitive, interpretive, and strategic therapies. Therapists were encouraged to develop hypotheses on the meaning of a patient's symptoms, which then informed the therapy. The symptoms were often seen as playing an important role in solving problems in adolescent development and in relationships with the family and others. Weight was an important focus of discussion, and the effects of prolonged self-starvation on mood and thinking were stressed. It was striking how a patient's body weight influenced the type of therapy possible: If the patient remained at a low body weight, a therapeutic alliance was difficult to establish; as the patient gained weight, the relationship with the therapist changed and a productive working partnership could be established.

Results

Results are only available for the whole group for the first year after the start of treatment. The random allocation resulted in the assignment of 41 patients to family therapy and 39 patients to individual therapy. Matching these two populations was known to be important and was thoroughly examined within each of the prognostic groups. Thus the patients were compared for weight loss, duration of illness, age at onset, and severity of symptoms, and their families were compared for EE ratings. There were no significant differences between the groups except for one—the patients allocated to family therapy had a shorter admission (mean 8.8 weeks) than those allocated to individual therapy (mean 12.1 weeks).

This did not seem to reflect systematically any aspect of the inpatient treatment practice and is likely to be a chance finding. The comparison of the effects of family therapy and the control treatment is confined to 73 of the 80 patients. The loss of 7 patients arises because they rejected the offer of treatment immediately after discharge from the hospital: 5 had been offered family therapy, and 2 had been offered individual therapy. The 73 remaining patients were all treated for a substantial number of sessions. Nevertheless, many of them did not complete the year of treatment. The possible influence on the results of these patients dropping out at different stages of the trial is discussed later. The results presented here were obtained from the main group of 73 patients.

Effects Measured by Categories of General Outcome

General outcome categories were defined as follows:

1. *Good outcome.* Body weight is maintained within 15% of the average body weight according to actuarial tables, and menstrual cycles are regular.
2. *Intermediate outcome.* Body weight has risen to within 15% of the average body weight, but amenorrhea persists.
3. *Poor outcome.* The patient is more than 15% below the average body weight or has developed bulimic symptoms.

For patients in the anorexia nervosa and bulimia nervosa group, the definitions were modified as follows:

1. *Good outcome.* There are no bulimic symptoms (no episodic overeating or self-induced vomiting); body weight is maintained within 15% of the average body weight.
2. *Intermediate outcome.* Bulimic symptoms are present but occur less frequently than once per week, and body weight is within 15% of the average body weight.
3. *Poor outcome.* Bulimic symptoms occur more frequently than once per week or body weight is less than 15% of the average body weight in the presence of less frequent symptoms.

Table 2 shows the distribution of the patients among the three categories of outcome (good, intermediate, and poor), according to each mode of treatment (family therapy or individual therapy) as it occurred within each of the four prognostic groups.

Early onset, short history. Family therapy was significantly superior to individual therapy. Six of the 10 patients in family therapy had a good outcome, compared with only 1 of the 11 patients in individual therapy ($P < .02$, using Fisher's exact probability test). When the patients with good and intermediate outcomes are counted together, 9 of the 10 patients in family therapy had the more favorable outcome, compared with only 2 of the 11 patients in individual therapy ($P < .002$).

Late onset. Table 2 shows that individual therapy was slightly favored, with a good outcome for 2 of 7 patients, compared with 0 of 7 patients in family therapy. This difference was not statistically significant, however.

Early onset, long history, and anorexia nervosa with bulimia nervosa. The distribution of the patients among the three general outcome categories was almost identical, whether they were in family therapy or individual therapy.

Table 2. Family therapy versus individual therapy: results after 1 year

Group	Therapy	General outcome		
		Good	Intermediate	Poor
Onset <18 years, duration <3 years	Family	6	3	1
	Individual	1	1	9
Onset <18 years, duration >3 years	Family	2	2	6
	Individual	2	1	6
Onset >19 years	Family	0	1	6
	Individual	2	1	4
Anorexia nervosa and bulimia nervosa	Family	0	1	8
	Individual	1	2	7

Effects Measured by Clinical Scales and Average Outcome Score

The 1-year follow-up assessment was compared with the assessment on entry into the trial using the individual Morgan and Russell scales. They provided measurements of change along the five clinical dimensions (nutritional, menstrual, mental state, psychosexual, and socioeconomic) and a general measure of progress from the average outcome score—the mean of the five scales.

Early onset, short history. In four of the five clinical dimensions (nutritional, menstrual, psychosexual, and socioeconomic), the patients receiving family therapy showed a significantly greater improvement than the patients receiving individual therapy (ranging from $P < .02$ to $P < .001$). A comparison of the two therapies on the average outcome scores also shows a better result for family therapy (family therapy, 9.7 + 2.8; individual therapy, 5.7 + 2.0; $P < .001$).

Effects Measured by Changes in Body Weight

In the early-onset, short-history group, the family therapy group gained more weight at 1 year compared with admission weight (25.6%) than did the individual therapy group (15.3%; $P < .01$). The advantage of family therapy was also evident when the weights at 1 year were compared with the discharge weights ($P < .02$): The weights of the family therapy patients were higher than their weights on discharge (+3.4%), whereas the weights of the individual therapy patients were still below the discharge levels (−8.3%). At 1 year, the mean weight of the family therapy group was 92.8% (± 8.4) compared with the average; in the individual therapy group it was 80.1% (± 15.1).

Also noteworthy was a comparison of patients who succeeded in maintaining their weight (more than 85% of the average body weight) from the time of discharge from the hospital. In the early-onset, short-history group, 5 of 10 patients in family therapy did so, compared to only 1 of 11 patients in individual therapy ($P < .05$).

In the late-onset group, the effects of the two therapies were reversed. Individual therapy was associated with a significantly greater weight gain when comparing levels at 1 year with those on admission (20.0%). The gain for patients in family therapy was 5.4% ($P < .01$). At 1 year, the mean weight for the individual therapy group was 79.9% (13.1), that for the family therapy group was 71.1% (8.3).

The effects of the two therapies did not differ significantly on any measure of weight in the early-onset, long-history and anorexia nervosa and bulimia nervosa groups.

Readmissions

Twenty-two patients required readmission during the year of outpatient therapy: 9 of 36 patients in family therapy (25%) and 13 of 37 patients in individual therapy (35%). This difference failed to reach statistical significance. The number of readmissions in each prognostic group was too small for analysis within groups.

Dropping Out of Treatment

Types of dropouts and their distribution. The treatment dropouts were classified as follows:

1. *Refusers*—7 patients who refused further treatment after discharge from the hospital (5 destined for family therapy and 2 for individual therapy).
2. *Early dropouts*—8 patients who defected within 3 months of therapy.
3. *Late dropouts*—13 patients who defected at any time after 3 months of therapy.

The overall rate of dropping out of treatment was similar for the two therapies: 15 of 41 for family therapy and 13 of 39 for individual therapy; however, significant differences were found in the early-onset, short-history and late-onset groups. There was a greater tendency for patients in the early-onset, short-history group to drop out of treatment if they had been allocated to individual therapy (7 of 11) rather than family therapy (1 of 10; $P < .02$, counting all three categories of dropping out). The reverse occurred in the late-onset group; none of the patients in individual therapy dropped out, whereas 4 of 8 did in family therapy ($P < .05$). These findings may be associated with the patients' ages. Patients older than 18 years tended to remain in treatment if it was individual rather than family therapy ($P < .03$); among patients of age 18 or younger, family therapy was the more acceptable treatment ($P < .04$).

Effects of dropping out on outcome results. To what extent did dropping out of treatment bias the results in favor of one or the other therapy? The first approach to answering this question was whether the patients who dropped out had poorer outcomes. There was some evidence that they fared less well, but this association was only demonstrable on a few measures. Taking the whole population, the average outcome score was higher for the "engaged" patients (7.38) than for the early and late dropouts combined (6.22; $P < .05$). Moreover, the number of months during which the patients maintained their weight higher than 85% of the average body weight averaged 5.40 for the 49 engaged anorexic patients, compared with 1.07 months for 7 early dropouts and refusers ($P < .03$).

The second approach to the influence of dropping out on the results was to reanalyze the results after exclusion of the early dropouts.

1. *Early onset, short history.* Family therapy was still significantly superior to individual therapy, using the most sensitive measures: the categories of general outcome ($P < .01$), the average outcome score ($P < .01$), and changes in body weight (weight gain at the end of the 1-year follow-up assessment was 25.4% with family therapy and 17.5% with individual therapy; [$P < .05$]).
2. *Late onset.* There was only one early dropout to be excluded from the previous analysis, and the previous finding still held a greater weight gain with individual therapy (20.0%) than with family therapy (3.9%) at the end of the 1-year follow-up assessment ($P < .01$).

It may thus be concluded that patients dropping out from treatment did not bias the direction of the main findings.

Frequency of Therapy Sessions

Although it was planned for frequency of sessions to be similar for both therapies, patients in family therapy had fewer sessions; means ± standard errors were 10.5 ± 8.9 for family therapy and 15.9 ± 8.5 for individual therapy. These differences reflected the practical problems of arranging frequent family sessions compared with generally easier arrangements for individual sessions.

Conclusion

This concludes the presentation of the major results of the treatment trial at 1-year follow-up. There are two further areas of interest, since the roles of family variables seem prominent. These concern factors associated with dropping out of treatment and factors predicting outcome at 1-year follow-up.

Factors Associated With Dropping Out of Treatment

Factors associated with dropping out of treatment were examined during the study when 27% of the first 51 patients were noted to have dropped out of treatment within 3 months of discharge from the hospital (Szmukler et al. 1985). Many factors possibly associated with dropping out were examined, including patient's age, age at onset, duration of illness, previous treatment, admission weight, patient's desired weight, discharge weight, and scores on the Morgan and Russell scales at admission. No patient variable was significantly associated with dropping out. The only predictor was parental EE, especially critical comments. There was, however, evidence of an important interaction between EE and the type of therapy offered. The relationship between EE and the type of therapy for the entire group of patients is shown in Table 3. High maternal EE is only associated with dropping out when family therapy was the treatment. Only maternal EE is presented, since nearly all high-EE fathers were married to high-EE mothers. Note that EE, as discussed in this chapter, is

Table 3. Expressed emotion (EE) and dropouts

	Dropout	Engaged
All patients[a]		
Low-EE mother	4	34
High-EE mother	9	16
Family therapy patients[b]		
Low-EE mother	1	20
High-EE mother	8	4
Individual therapy patients[c]		
Low-EE mother	3	14
High-EE mother	1	12

[a]$\chi = 6.00$; $P = .02$. [b]$\chi = 14.75$; $P = .0001$. [c]P of χ^2 is not significant.

based on critical comments (≥ 6) alone. Emotional overinvolvement did not add significantly to predictive power.

There was also an interaction between EE and the presence of bulimic symptoms in the patient. If these symptoms occurred, it was significantly more likely ($P = .02$) for the mother to have high EE (11 of 18 versus 14 of 45). A patient with bulimia was also more likely to drop out of therapy, although this just failed to reach statistical significance ($P = .09$). Thus it appears that dropping out of treatment was determined by an interaction between EE and family therapy, with some contribution from whether the patient was bulimic.

There were other interesting features of EE, which were noted by Szmukler et al. (1985). These include significant correlations between mothers' and fathers' scores on each of the scales and the suggestion of a relationship with social class—higher EE being associated with higher socioeconomic status. The relationship with social class may be due in part to a greater degree of disappointment in daughters by parents who had greater expectations of their success.

Predictors of Outcome at 1 Year

At the end of the 1-year follow-up assessment, we looked at whether there were factors noted at admission that might have pointed to a good or poor outcome at 1 year and whether they were influenced by the type of treatment offered.

Only one variable on a simple univariate analysis showed a relationship to outcome. This was the patient's discharge weight prior to entering the outpatient phase of treatment. The higher the discharge weight (as percentage of average body weight), the better the eventual outcome in terms of the general outcome score ($F = 7.19$ with 2 df; $P = .001$). A group of other measures, however, showed an important set of interactions in their association with general outcome: prognostic group, parental EE, and type of therapy.

As in the discussion on dropping out, the measure of parental EE is based on mothers' critical comments (≥ 6) alone. Emotional overinvolvement added little to the predictive power of the EE measure, as nearly all mothers with high emotional overinvolvement were also critical. Fathers' EE also added little, since 12 of 16 high-EE fathers (≥ 3 critical comments) also had high-EE wives.

The best outcome occurred in the early-onset, short-history group

(Group 1) when family therapy was the treatment. In addition, this group of patients had low-EE parents (only 3 of 21 families had a high-EE mother). Good and intermediate outcomes are treated as a single group because of the small numbers of subjects. High-EE parents were nearly all found in Groups 2, 3, and 4 (early onset, long history; late onset; anorexia nervosa and bulimia nervosa)—that is, in those groups including patients with chronic illnesses, in which the patients were older, or in which bulimia was the major feature. Tables 4 and 5 summarize these findings.

Table 6 demonstrates a relationship between EE and outcome that is accounted for entirely in the family therapy group. High EE is associated with a poor outcome when the treatment is family therapy but not when it is individual therapy.

Table 6 possibly suggests that family therapy with a high-EE family is associated with a poorer outcome than individual therapy with a member of such a family. A poor outcome was noted in 11 of 12 cases of family therapy in families with a high-EE mother and in 8 of 13 cases with individual therapy ($P = .05$). This conclusion is dubious, however, as patients from high-EE families were not randomly assigned to the treatments. In fact, the family therapy group had more patients from the late-onset group, whereas the individual therapy group had more patients from the early-onset, long-history group; both therapy groups had the same number of patients with bulimia nervosa. The situation is further complicated

Table 4. Expressed emotion (EE) and prognostic groups

| | Prognostic group | |
	Group 1	Groups 2–4
Low-EE mother	17	21
High-EE mother	3	22

Note.   Group 1, early onset, short history; Group 2, early onset, long history; Group 3, late onset; Group 4, anorexia nervosa and bulimia nervosa. $\chi = 7.46$; $P = .006$.

Table 5. Outcome and prognostic groups

| | Outcome | |
	Good/intermediate	Poor
Group 1	11	10
Groups 2–4	16	42

Note.   Group 1, early onset, short history; Group 2, early onset, long history; Group 3, late onset; Group 4, anorexia nervosa and bulimia nervosa. $\chi = 4.21$; $P = .04$.

Table 6. Expressed emotion (EE) and outcome

	Outcome	
	Good/intermediate	Poor
All patients[a]		
Low-EE mother	17	21
High-EE mother	6	19
Family therapy patients[b]		
Low-EE mother	13	8
High-EE mother	1	11
Individual therapy patients[c]		
Low-EE mother	4	13
High-EE mother	5	8

[a]$\chi = 2.80$; $P = .09$. [b]$\chi = 8.97$; $P = .003$. [c]$\chi = .78$; P is not significant.

by treatment dropouts, as noted before, with a strong relationship between mothers' EE and dropping out of treatment in the family therapy group but not in the individual therapy group.

Implications of the Study

To interpret the results reasonably, some methodological issues need to be mentioned. First, patients participating in this treatment trial were selected for severe illnesses and chronicity. The Maudsley Hospital is often a secondary or tertiary referral center for patients with eating disorders, and most patients have failed in treatment elsewhere before seeking therapy at Maudsley. Caution must be exercised in generalizing the results of this study. A different pattern of outcome would be likely in a center serving a different population of patients, such as that associated with a children's or adolescent unit. The findings in this study are consistent with those reported by Minuchin et al. (1975) and Martin (1985), who dealt with the early-onset, short-history spectrum of patients.

Second, therapist enthusiasm for family therapy might have accounted for the better results for family therapy. When this study was conducted, there was a vogue for family therapy, and individual therapy was probably less discussed and excited less interest. This factor was probably not of major significance because individual therapy produced a better outcome in the late-onset group, the opposite of what would have been predicted if therapist enthusiasm was a major factor.

Third, research design may have led to an artificial dichotomy of treatments; in real life, a combination of individual and family therapies might prove most appropriate. Whether such a combination of treatments would prove more effective than either treatment alone merits further investigation.

Finally, it remains to be seen whether the benefit of family therapy seen at 1-year follow-up will also be evident in the longer-term outcome, for example, at 4 years or later. At the very least, however, it is clear that the duration of the illness may be significantly shortened by family therapy in some patients.

Within the aforementioned constraints, it may thus be concluded that the study provides good evidence that family therapy is the preferable short-term treatment for young patients with anorexia nervosa when the illness is not chronic. For older patients, those with a chronic illness, or those with anorexia nervosa and bulimia nervosa (severe enough to warrant hospitalization), however, family therapy failed to demonstrate any benefit. If anything (the findings here were far from conclusive), patients in the late-onset group benefited more from individual supportive psychotherapy.

A major family variable, EE, was examined and shown to influence both dropping out of treatment and the outcome at 1-year follow-up. The meaning of high EE in terms of family functioning has not been formally studied, and it remains essentially an empirical measure with useful predictive properties. Leff and Vaughn (1985) discussed the possible associations of high EE in terms of family interactions. One study (Miklowitz et al. 1984) showed significant associations between EE and ratings on another instrument, "affective style," based on transcriptions of videotaped family interactions involving an adolescent patient. High-EE patients (based largely on critical comments) were more likely to score high on criticisms, both "benign" and "harsh," in direct interaction with the patient on the affective-style measure. In another study (Szmukler et al. 1987), we demonstrated that the most important component of the measure, critical comments, shows a high correlation between the conventional individual setting in which a parent is interviewed alone and a family setting involving a videotaped "picnic lunch" in which both parents and siblings are present. The correlation was .80 for the rating of critical comments, which was highly statistically significant. Correlations on the other components of EE were more modest.

Leff and Vaughn (1985) attempted to describe the differences between high- and low-EE relatives based on impressions from the many interviews they have performed. Most of the families included a schizophrenic patient. Low-EE relatives were thought more respectful of the patient's relationship needs; for example, they adapted more readily to the patient's demands for either greater reassurance and support or increased social distance. High-EE relatives appeared more intrusive, monitoring the patient's activities inappropriately and not respecting his or her need for privacy. High-EE parents also seemed less convinced that the patient's behavior was caused by illness and were more likely to perceive it as indicating "badness." They appeared less able to empathize with and understand the patient's abnormal experiences. Perhaps related to this was the low-EE relatives' lowering of expectations concerning what the patient was capable of doing, whereas high-EE relatives seemed unable to make allowances for impaired performance.

Hooley (1985), also on the basis of interviews with relatives of schizophrenic patients, formed the impression that high-EE parents were attempting to exert control over apparent uncontrollable behavior of a patient. This particularly seemed to apply to behavior not obviously caused by florid psychotic symptoms, such as delusions and hallucinations, but to that related to the "negative" symptoms of schizophrenia, such as apathy or anergia, where it might appear that the patient could be trying harder.

Some of these features are of particular relevance to patients with schizophrenia in whom an optimal level of arousal is believed to result in optimal functioning. These patients are believed to be especially vulnerable to high levels of arousal, which will likely lead to a relapse if arousal exceeds a certain threshold. For patients with anorexia nervosa, the mechanisms whereby such parental characteristics lead to a poorer outcome appear less obvious. It is also important that in our study EE was only relevant to outcome when family therapy was the treatment offered. Our impression was that high-EE relatives felt most heavily burdened by their daughter's illness and perhaps the most guilty. Being asked to participate in family therapy must have seemed like adding insult to injury; instead of the mental health professionals accepting the task of making their daughters better, it might have appeared to the parents that they were being asked to do it. This must have reinforced their sense of burden and their guilt, since this form of therapy could imply that they were doing something wrong that was causing their daughter's illness.

Hooley's (1985) observations may also have some relevance in that many uncontrollable behaviors by anorexic patients (such as not eating) could be perceived as caused by the patient not trying hard enough. A parent whose usual means of coping is through attempts to control the interactions and behavior of another might be more likely to be critical and perhaps more threatened by a treatment focusing on family interactions. Approaches to therapy that aimed to counteract these forces are described in Chapter 2.

Fairly early in the trial, we became especially aware of the issue of dropping out and its potential in making the treatment trial inconclusive. Much attention in the latter part of the study was devoted to the process of engagement in family therapy and, to a lesser degree, individual therapy. The details of the methods employed are described in Chapter 2, but we can mention here that there was evidence that these met with some degree of success. Fourteen of 51 patients dropped out of treatment within the first 3 months in the earlier part of the study, but this number fell to 1 of 29 patients in the latter part of the study. This evidence is not wholly conclusive, however, since there were fewer high-EE parents in the latter period.

References

Hooley JM: Expressed emotion: a review of the critical literature. Clinical Psychology Review 5:119–139, 1985

Leff J, Vaughn C: The interaction of life events and relatives' expressed emotion in schizophrenia and depressive neurosis. Br J Psychiatry 136:146–153, 1980

Leff J, Vaughn C: Expressed Emotion in Families. New York, Guilford, 1985

Martin FE: The treatment and outcome of anorexia nervosa in adolescents: a prospective study and five year follow-up. J Psychiatr Res 19:509–514, 1985

Miklowitz DJ, Goldstein MJ, Falloon IRH, et al: International correlates of expressed emotion in the families of schizophrenics. Br J Psychiatry 144:482–487, 1984

Minuchin S, Baker L, Rosman BL, et al: A conceptual model of psychosomatic illness in children: family organization and family therapy. Arch Gen Psychiatry 32:1031–1038, 1975

Morgan HG, Russell GFM: Value of family background and clinical feature as predictors of long-term outcome in anorexia nervosa: four year follow-up study of 41 patients. Psychol Med 5:355–371, 1975

Russell GFM, Szmukler GI, Eisler I, et al: An evaluation of family therapy in anorexia nervosa and bulimia nervosa. Arch Gen Psychiatry 44:1047–1056, 1987

Szmukler GI, Russell GFM: Outcome and prognosis of anorexia nervosa, in Handbook of Eating Disorders. Edited by Brownell KD, Foreyt JP. New York, Basic Books, 1986, pp 283–300

Szmukler GI, Eisler I, Russell GFM, et al: Anorexia nervosa, parental "expressed emotion" and dropping out of treatment. Br J Psychiatry 147:265–271, 1985

Szmukler GI, Berkovits R, Eisler I, et al: A comparative study of parental "expressed emotion" in individual and family settings. Br J Psychiatry 151:174–178, 1987

Chapter 2

Family Therapy of Early-Onset, Short-History Anorexia Nervosa

CHRISTOPHER DARE, M.D., M.R.C.P., D.P.M., F.R.C.Psych.
GEORGE SZMUKLER, M.D., D.P.M., F.R.C.Psych., F.R.A.N.Z.C.P.

Chapter 2

Family Therapy of Early-Onset, Short-History Anorexia Nervosa

*I*n Chapter 1, we described the evidence from a controlled trial that family therapy has an attested part to play in the management of anorexia nervosa—the treatment of patients with early-onset, short-history anorexia nervosa (Dare et al., in press; Russell et al. 1987).

We have some evidence from a partially controlled retrospective survey of two samples—one treated in outpatient family therapy, the other by admission to an adolescent unit—that family therapy is as effective as inpatient treatment for early-onset, short-history anorexia nervosa (Dare 1983). In addition to these two studies, we have abundant clinical evidence that family therapy can render inpatient admission of young anorexia nervosa patients unnecessary. By means of family therapy, we find that, in many cases, we are successful in helping parents take short-term but effective control of their child's diet. This regularly (but by no means inevitably) leads to the return of the patient to physical and psychological well-being, and his or her expected level of socialization can be achieved. We are undertaking a prospective controlled trial of two forms of outpatient family therapy to explore in more detail the effectiveness of different elements in family therapy and to investigate the quality of psychological changes in the patient and family. A pilot survey preliminary to the larger study has shown that different *forms* of family intervention can be clinically successful, although whether equally so we do not know. Study of the 18 patients in this pilot trial, however, has given us further evidence of the *nature* of successful family therapy. We have established some family and individual measures that predict outcome at a point 6 months after the inception of the treatment program for patients with anorexia nervosa in family therapy (C. Dare, I. Eisler, and D. LeGrange, 1989, unpublished observations).

Although the emphasis in this chapter is on work with the families of adolescent patients, we have not given up family therapy with older patients. This is justified, first, because there are no clearly reliable successful treatments for late-onset and longer-enduring anorexia nervosa and, second, because an anorexic patient and his or her family often stay in close contact well into young adulthood and beyond. Moreover, it is extremely common for families of older patients to have a strong involvement in the symptomatic behavior.

These factors can also be true for bulimic patients, from whom evidence for effective family therapy is also notably lacking. Successful family treatment for bulimia nervosa has been reported (Madanes 1981; Wynne 1980), and in our own clinical experience we have recorded some satisfactory cases; however, this chapter does not address family therapy for bulimic patients.

Historical Development of Family Intervention in Anorexia Nervosa

There are frequent early references to the clinical importance of the parents of anorexic patients (e.g., Charcot 1889; Gull 1874; Lasègue 1873; Ryle 1936). They have been commented on by family therapists, giving historical precedent for their own focus (Dare 1985; Minuchin et al. 1978; Selvini-Palazzoli 1974). In the early accounts, mostly by physicians, the mother and father of the anorexic patient are portrayed as intensely preoccupied with the patient's treatment and are seen as having the potential to sabotage the management of the treatment. For this reason, it was advised that parents should be separated from the patient during treatment ("parentectomy"), as if to detoxify a person with noxious influence. These physicianly approaches were not subject to specific or detailed investigation. With the rise of psychoanalytic perspective on anorexia nervosa (Lorand 1943; Masserman 1941; Thoma 1967; Waller et al.

1940), however, a more elaborate view of the parents was evoked. This psychoanalytic perspective detailed intricately the experience of the patient-mother relationship, particularly from the patient's point of view. It reached its apogee in the work of Bruch (1974), who emphasized the difficulty of the anorexic patient in gaining a sense of being an independent person from her mother. In an interesting three-generational study, Blitzer et al. (1961) identified problems in the mother's own feeding experience, with the maternal grandmother as a precursor and progenitor of the anorexic patient's eating disorder. The psychoanalytic studies, like those of the physicians, tended to cast the parents in the roles of malign influences on their daughter's psychological development. This was the heyday of the "psychopathogenic" mother. The model of intervention for this view was, ultimately, that the mother needed psychotherapy to change her "neurotic" or "characterological" need to be so intrusive and oppressive. The father, insofar as he was mentioned in the psychoanalytic literature, was often described as cold, distant, and absorbed in his career (Thoma 1967), "etiologically" relevant as such but not implicated in a treatment program.

Family therapy has a direct lineage from the psychoanalytic studies. Indeed, Selvini-Palazzoli's (1974) work with anorexic patients describes the evolutions of her view—first as a psychoanalytic psychotherapist and then as a family-system therapist. Minuchin (1970) also developed his therapy for families from a psychoanalytic background. Therefore, it is not surprising that both authors incorporate some of the psychoanalytic insights about family dynamics and the psychology of anorexia nervosa into their work. Summaries of the evolution and integration of the psychoanalytic and family-system perspectives were provided by Yager (1982) and Dare (1985). The importance of the more recent family-system approach is that it establishes therapeutic tools, whereas the earlier tendency had been for theories of family involvement to provide only scapegoats. Nonetheless, there remains a danger that family-system thinking substitutes blaming the family for blaming the mother.

The achievements of family therapy should not be taken as endorsements of a theory of family causation of severe eating disorder. On the contrary, therapeutic success with family therapy may require specific disavowal of belief in family etiology.

Selvini-Palazzoli and Minuchin founded important and influential schools of family therapy theory and practice. Selvini-Palazzoli and her associates in Milan have had an international, evolving, and now-divergent impact. The particular constructions about the nature of family life and family history in anorexic patients described in the 1970s (Selvini-Palazzoli 1974) have changed. The suggestions for therapeutic procedures have also changed. Minuchin and his colleagues produced coherent accounts of family processes and family therapy in anorexia nervosa (Minuchin et al. 1975, 1978; Sargent et al. 1985), which are part of the corpus of structural family therapy. The principles and practices of this form of family therapy can be more easily codified, and they have probably been more easily integrated into a common ground of "eclectic" family therapy. Several other less precisely labeled family therapists have published accounts of patients with anorexia nervosa (Martin 1985; Stern et al. 1981; White 1983).

Minuchin et al. (1975, 1978) and Martin (1985) presented the proportion of successes and failures of their treatments, but their series were uncontrolled. There were probably considerable differences between the techniques of Martin and Minuchin, but there were also certain commonalities. (Martin acknowledges the influence of the Philadelphia Child Guidance Group.) There is a marked absence of controlled trials, comparisons of different forms of family therapy, and even follow-up studies of some of the clinical studies mentioned here. Therefore, any descriptions claiming efficacy for particular aspects of family therapy must be treated with caution. In this chapter, we describe the therapy used in our treatment trials and clinical practice. Where possible, we indicate the links between what we do and the procedures described by other authors in the field.

Generalizations about what goes on in families are often confusing. The language of and the level of abstraction or interpretation in the descriptions make comparisons between different descriptions complicated. It is not clear, for example, whether Selvini-Palazzoli's original descriptions of the three-generational rigidities and loyalties complement or contradict Minuchin's concept of rigidity and intergenerational triangulations in families with anorexic patients. Similarly, Stern et al. (1981) succinctly evoked the problem of separation and individuation of anorexic patients at adolescence. This seems related to but not the same as Minuchin's accounts of the enmeshment of families with anorexic patients. Minuchin's descriptions (rigidity, enmeshment, overprotectiveness, problems of conflict resolution, triangulation) are, in principle, those of observable family interactions. Attempts to make these qualities operational to produce measurements have been (surprisingly to us) unsuccessful (Kog et al. 1985). Selvini-Palazzoli (1974) and White (1983) described intergenerationally transmitted family attitudes and belief systems—manifest in expressed views and behaviors but with a less clearly specified relationship between belief and observable behavior. The importance of these generalizations about family processes is that they are, openly or covertly, the targets of family treatment. Family therapists, like most psychotherapists, write as though there is a congruence of the subject matter or target of treatment and technique. For instance, Minuchin et al. (1978) described the qualities of psychosomatic families and then addressed the possibilities of particularly therapeutic interventions for the different qualities. As we argue elsewhere (Dare et al. 1990), this procedure may be misleading. Although we find Minuchin's descriptions illuminating and convincing accounts of what goes on in many families containing a patient with an eating disorder, the relationship to treatment is much less demonstrable.

Different theoretical models linking description and intervention are possible. Take a single quality—overprotectiveness—as an example. Its presence in families with anorexic patients could have several possible implications: 1) Overprotectiveness might, in theory, be a response to the presence of an ill child in a "normal" family and might diminish as the child improves and requires no specific intervention. 2) Persistent overprotectiveness after the child improves may merely require straightforward information about counseling. 3) Although it is an outcome of self-starvation, overprotectiveness may feed on the symptoms and need to be diminished to help the patient improve. 4) Overprotectiveness could, in theory, antedate and be pathogenic for eating disorders, but it could also be unimportant and not require treatment. 5) Overprotectiveness might be a major factor leading to the development and maintenance of the anorexic symptoms and must therefore be eliminated in the treatment of the condition.

There is no evidence about the actual place of familial overprotectiveness in the pathogenesis or maintenance of anorexic symptoms. In our studies, the closest we have come to finding a measure of overprotectiveness is the emotional-overinvolvement element in the expressed emotion studies of Leff and Vaughn (1985). We found that this element is generally at a low level and its quantitative presence does not predict the course of anorexia nervosa (Szmukler et al. 1985a, 1985b, 1987). We are beginning to suspect that another element of expressed emotion—critical comments—relates to the problems that Minuchin described as conflict resolution. We now have evidence that critical comments are at a low level in the families of patients with eating disorders (C. Dare, I. Eisler, and D. LeGrange, 1989, unpublished observations). Even slightly raised levels (two or more critical comments) predict a poor outcome for anorexic patients treated by family therapy. This relationship may not hold for patients treated by individual therapy. We have tentative evidence that family therapy for anorexia nervosa will be unsuccessful in those families in which the parents, during formal testing, express two or more critical comments concerning their child's eating disorder unless the therapy is successful in reducing the critical comments (Dare et al. 1989, unpublished observations).

We know of no studies that attempt to elucidate the relationship between targets and interventions in any of the other forms of family therapy advocated for anorexia nervosa. The absence of more detailed knowledge about the targets of family therapy and specific predictors of the symptomatic state of the patient must limit the value of all accounts of family therapy. Nevertheless, the clinical experiences of some therapists (Selvini-Palazzoli 1974; Stern et al. 1981; White 1983) in the management of anorexia nervosa cannot be dismissed. The wisdom and acumen of their clinical descriptions of the families are matched by the ingenuity and breadth of their treatment strategies and techniques.

First Phase: Setting Up Treatment

Relationship Between Establishment of Family Therapy and Inpatient Care

In the early days of our involvement with the families of adolescents with eating disorders, the patients were routinely admitted to hospitals. Rotrok et al. (1977) showed the advantages of adding family therapy to the treatment programs of an adolescent inpatient unit, but there are particular difficulties for the family therapist conducting whole-family therapy when the patient is also involved with many members of a multidisciplinary team. As the family has contact with other members of the hospital staff, as well as with the family therapist, the family can inadvertently or deliberately elicit information that contradicts or subverts the therapist's interventions. Other staff members may develop attitudes and beliefs about the parents that are communicated to the patient and that obstruct the aim of the family therapist however well and frequently the multidisciplinary team and family therapist communicate. The timing of visits home and discharge are determined by ward structures and dynamics, and these may counteract processes in the family therapy.

In our reported trial, all patients were admitted to the hospital, but family therapy began after discharge, the therapist having met patient and family shortly before then. In more routine practice, at least half of the adolescent patients have been admitted under the care of physicians, pediatricians, and psychologists before referral to the family therapy team. Many of these patients are still inpatients at referral.

Convening the First Meeting

The family therapist must decide, in the light of the overall context of treatment, when first to meet the problem, whom to meet, and what the physical nature of the therapeutic setting should be.

Our prescription for these matters follows. The family therapist should begin by requiring the whole family to attend a consultation in the family therapist's setting. To do this is usually easy, but it may require firmness, tact, and some guile. Parents and child may wish to be seen alone at first, and the therapist (while not discounting such meetings or possibilities) should say that a whole-family consultation is the best way to begin, "in my experience of this difficult and dangerous problem." The therapist should insist on this (in the light of the specific information already provided and from general experiences) and emphasize the family's particular circumstances and the therapist's authority. The parents may object that their daughter does not want to talk in their presence. The therapist should accept that the parents will not be able to make their child talk in the family meeting but add, for example, the following: "You must be able to make her come. If your child is legally an infant [younger than 18 years of age in Great Britain], then you, as the parents, have a legal duty to ensure that she gets proper treatment. It's tough, but you have to be able to do it. Tell her I won't let her talk if she does not feel it to be right." The parents will want to know whom to bring, and should be told that, to gain a proper view of the problem, the therapist will need to see, at a minimum, all of the people in the patient's household. Grown siblings who have left home are extremely valuable allies and informants in treatment. The parents should be told this and asked to invite them to the meeting as well. As independent adults, however, their attendance cannot be made a condition of treatment. Grown siblings who are still in the household may wish to be exempt, have to work, or have study demands, and their presence may not be wanted by the patient. For the first interview, the therapist should require their presence, saying to the parents, for example, "You are head of your household. You have a frightening problem to deal with, and you can *ask* for the support and loyalty of your children. They will surely wish to do something for you at this time, during this crisis."

In one-third of our referrals, the parents are separated or divorced and most have remarried. This requires consideration as to who should attend. First, the custodial parent and his or her household should be invited. If the patient has staying access to the other parent and that household, then those individuals will probably have to be seen at a separate or combined meeting. Nonparental spouses or cohabitees should always be seen. Both biological parents will be needed in therapy if they both preside over meals with the patient. The nonbiological parents must not experience the therapy as reconvening the former marriage but as developing effective coparenting skills to cope with the crisis in their child.

Throughout these preliminary telephone contacts, the therapist has two aims: to establish that there is a crisis and to begin a process of defining and enhancing parental authority of a special order as being necessary to surmount the crisis. The process of enhancing parental authority is in accordance with Minuchin's suggestions about defining and clarifying hierarchical structures. The focus on the state of crisis is related to Stanton's (1981) felicitous term "compression." Both notions derive from the practice of the Philadelphia Child Guidance Clinic. The tone and quality of the therapist's communications are influenced by strategic therapists such as Haley (1976, 1980) and Madanes (1981).

Even if the patient is in the hospital, attendance at the family therapy is required. The therapist needs to feel maximally secure and familiar in the treatment context and to have the regular support of team and technical backup available. The quality and extent of the backup required depend on the therapist's level of experience. The more experienced the therapist (working with families in general and patients with eating disorders in particular), the less familiarity and technical support become important. For a relatively inexperienced therapist, the support team helps identify crucial family processes and devise treatment strategies and is especially important. Few therapists should aim to work completely without a one-way screen or colleagues in the room at certain points in difficult therapies for patients with eating disorders. Video facilities are essential for training and for certain research techniques whereby family processes and treatments are rated by blind assessors.

For experienced family therapists unused to working with patients with eating disorders, an observing clinician familiar with the physiology, psychology, and family processes related to self-starvation, binge eating, vomiting, and purging is also an essential backup. Facilities to monitor weight, height, blood chemistry, and cardiac and endocrine status are minimal laboratory requirements, especially because the patient's discharge from an inpatient service should be an immediate goal for the family therapist. Of course, sometimes the threat to life delays this.

Joining and Engaging With Family

Family therapy is, on the whole, brief. Successful therapy with adolescent patients with eating disorders rarely takes more than 15 sessions spanning 8–14 months. (Unsuccessful treatments usually end after more sessions for a much longer time.) Effectiveness in so few meetings requires that the therapist establish a powerful contact and rapport with the patient's family.

The first face-to-face greeting should therefore be conducted intensely, gravely, empathically, warmly, sincerely, and portentously. A priest meeting the family of the bereaved at a funeral is a possible model. At the first greeting, the therapist should judge how much physical contact might be possible with each member of the family and then give just a bit more, holding a handshake longer, using two hands, putting an arm around a teenager, embracing little children, and lingering fearfully over the patient's gaunt body.

In a similar style, the family is then told of the observation and video link with the interviewing room, stressing how necessary these arrangements are for the therapist to help with the patient's serious predicament. This always gains the family's agreement to be observed. Confidentiality is ensured.

The family is then ceremoniously introduced to the consulting room, shown the television cameras and the one-way screen, and told about the invisible team of colleagues. Arrangements for an in-house physical evaluation will have been made before the therapist's arrival, and "evidence" of the patient's state will be in the treatment room—principally a weight chart. During subsequent interviews, the therapist should always weigh the patient (and often measure height if growth is predicted).

In the consulting room, the therapist then checks that each family member knows why the family is attending. The way in which the family members describe the problem influences the therapist's reflections back to the family, but the reflection amplifies the seriousness and focuses on the patient's physical danger and psychological distress and the family's sense of having done all it could to help, to no avail. The therapist's aim is to increase family anxiety as much as possible, given the realities of the life threat, the patient's weight, and the patient's preoccupation with body shape. At the same time, the therapist should be as warm, as friendly, as positive about the family, and as emotional as possible. If possible, the therapist should become genuinely imbued with the horror, despair, panic, and hopelessness of the family. These feelings should be expressed openly, unambiguously, and as peacefully as possible. The therapist must impress all family members with his or her wish to understand the patient's problem and how each family member feels about it.

As soon as possible, the therapist should orchestrate an intense scene that neither scapegoats the patient, blames the parents, nor exempts the siblings. All of those involved should be held focused on the horror. If the patient has been in the hospital and her weight has been restored, possible rapid weight loss after discharge should be emphasized. If the weight gain in the hospital was unsatisfactory, it should be grieved over. The inability of health care professionals to help the patient back to health should be established by history, without criticizing or deriding the professionals, who should be spoken of respectfully and admiringly. Their failure is a measure of the crisis and the extent to which the family is the last resort for the patient. The distance the family has traveled and what it has given up to attend should be used as evidence of the family's love, loyalty, commitment, and worry.

All of this information may perturb the patient. Often she fears that the problem is exaggerated. More often the true level of the patient's fear is being expressed, which she would rather not display to the family. The patient fears that the therapist is unleashing the family on her. The therapist should try to show the patient that her state of mind and her complex mixture of feelings can be expressed, accepted, and openly acknowledged. This is the most difficult aspect of the family therapy because the patient cannot usually imagine how anyone can understand her or—if her views are understood—how anyone could possibly want her to eat more or to gain weight. This task is especially difficult with patients who are very thin, miserable, withdrawn, and totally preoccupied with weight and diet. It is vital that the therapist show the family sympathy and understanding of the patient. Above all, the therapist must model a totally noncritical attitude toward the patient's symptoms. The therapist should abhor what has happened to the patient, how her life has been interrupted, how her freedom was taken from her, and how her independent development was curtailed. The therapist should show as much positive warmth for the patient and as much distress and fear about the symptoms as possible. This is necessary because, at all costs, the parental and sibling criticism of the patient and her symptoms should be counteracted, diminished, and modified. The therapist should seek to establish a sympathetic noncritical alliance with all family members while increasing their anxiety and their sense of taking on a dreadful task at which the professionals have failed.

The climax of the session is reached when the therapist gently but forcefully and relentlessly points out to the family that it will have to find a way to manage and, eventually, to control the patient's symptomatic behavior, making her eat, gain weight, recover menstruation, and stop binging, vomiting, and engaging in excessive exercise.

The family members become horrified. They have been trying to do nothing else for weeks and months. They cannot possibly do it. Why else would they have come to the family therapist? The therapist acknowledges the force of what they say but points out the lack of alternatives. Hospital admission to restore weight is possible, but subsequent weight loss is the more likely, almost inevitable, occurrence, and the family will once more be in the same predicament. With great sympathy and sorrow, the therapist ends the first session, asking the family to return soon, making an appointment for another session within a few days, to which the whole family will come again, this time with a picnic meal to be eaten with the therapist. The therapist enjoins the family to bring as much food for the patient as they think appropriate—not based on her wishes but on her starvation.

The therapist has attempted to engage the family by setting up what can be called a therapeutic bind. The authoritative stance with the family and about the eating disorder and the warmth and positive acceptance of the family should attach the family to the therapist. The confidence, conviction, and knowledge of the therapist is set beside the alarm and despair engendered in the family. Socially and customarily, those who raise anxiety are antagonistic, angry, critical, and hostile. The *bind* is the mixture of panic induction and loving warmth. If this mixture can be authentically and powerfully mobilized, the family will return with the picnic.

Assessing the Family

While with the family, the therapist will have been making many apprais-
als, assessing the mental state of the patient and the characters of all of
the family members (including the patient). Above all, the therapist will
have been observing the process of family interactions. The assessment of
the transactional organization of the family and the patterns of family life
will have been taking place at several different levels. At an interval during the first interview and after the end of the session, the therapist will
discuss his or her observations and assessments with the observing clinical team. We think that clinical observations of identifiable observer veri-
fiability can be made (Dare 1988; Szmukler et al. 1985a, 1985b), and this
process is enhanced by a consensual formulation. We recommend that
descriptions should clearly indicate the distinction between behavioral
and interactional observations and interpretative constructions about the
meaning and patterns of the interactional behavior.

If the therapist has been emotionally involved with the family, there
is a risk of imbalances and partiality in his or her assessment of the family. On the other hand, the way in which the therapist becomes absorbed
into the family provides information about how the family works. We
believe that our social training automatically leads us to accommodate
ourselves to the family pattern, adjusting our role and style to fit in with
the family. This is partly acceptable professionally, because it signifies to
the family that we are courteous and respectful. On the contrary, it is also
professionally hazardous. There is a risk that we will unconsciously fit in
with family patterns that render the family ineffective in overcoming the
patient's eating disorder. This is one reason for requiring an observing
team—to modify and develop the therapist's direct responses to the patient's family.

The family therapist needs to establish knowledge of the family
structure. This consists of the stable often-repeated patterns of communicating, controlling, nurturing, socializing, forming boundaries, making al-
liances and coalitions, and solving problems. These patterns and the affective coloring associated with them are elicited as the family copes with
meeting the therapist and responding to the bind that has been created.
The patterns also become obvious during the family meals, which provide strong exposure to the family's characteristic organization.

The therapist's knowledge of these patterns is important because the
therapy will have, as one aim, the effect of disrupting the familiar patterns of family life, at least temporarily. Minuchin et al. (1978) stated

categorically that the aim of family therapy is to change the family structure. We are unsure of that. We certainly agree that we can see patterns whereby the family's management of the eating disorder is demonstrably counterproductive. For example, when one parent takes on a firm, insistent stance, compelling the patient to eat, the other parent becomes an ally of the patient's symptoms, expressing the fear that the quantities of food are too great, the caloric content is too high, and the patient's stomach is too shrunk. The parents may reverse these roles, completely, within a few moments. The pattern is clear—a cross-generational instead of an interparental alliance. For now, we advocate that the therapist oppose many of the observed family structures, especially those that confuse communication, disrupt powerful parental control, obscure clear cross-generational boundaries, and interfere with the maintenance of clear separateness of identity. The therapist constantly encourages the discovery and practice of new patterns of family interactions by direct instructions and by the way in which he or she addresses the family and constructs the family meeting.

The therapist hopes to enforce change by disrupting old and familiar patterns, taking advantage of the family's disorientation in the strange setting of the family therapy unit and under the impact of the therapeutic bind.

The therapist's effectiveness in producing these changes is enhanced by the second type of understanding of the family—the formulation of the significance of the family patterns and the symptoms of the patient. Families have belief systems accounting for the qualities of personal relationships experienced by the family members. A belief system may amount to myths (Byng-Hall 1973, 1979) of the origins and formulations of the family. Such myths are part history and part interpretations and constructions that have been consequently developed to account for the qualities of family life. Clearly, beliefs about family life exist both consciously and subconsciously. For example, family members may be aware that no demands are ever made on the father to join the mother in ordering their daughter to eat more. The lack of such demands may reach the proportions of a taboo, which is accepted because the father feels extraordinarily guilty over the suicide of his sister in his young adulthood. His sister's death may or may not be known in the family. The father's intense nexus of feelings about young women threatening their own lives may be a powerful force in the family, aiding ineffective management of the symptomatic behavior. Unless the family therapist can access these types of family belief systems, the interventions that he or she makes will feel crass and inappropriate to the family.

The assessment of the family is not a single occurrence. Further and enriching understanding comes throughout the treatment.

Dealing With Symptoms

We do not think that symptoms are the outcome of a family's structural qualities, although we do observe that there are patterns of family interaction that render a family powerless in the face of symptoms. We do not think that the meanings attributed to the symptoms create the symptoms, but we do think that such belief systems must be understood and respected by the therapist. We do not think that a patient with an eating disorder can improve unless and until there is a change in the dietary pattern. Anorexic patients must gain weight to get better. These truisms are stated to establish that family therapy does not aim to be effective by its power to undo a hypothetical family etiology. Family therapy must change the way the family responds to and manages the symptomatic behavior. With adolescent patients, the aim is to enable the parents to set up a meal regimen, such as occurs in a well-functioning hospital inpatient unit for eating disorders. There must be a culture such that eating and completing a meal promptly occurs, because the expectation for that occurrence is relentlessly powerful. The culture created must be such that there is no alternative to compliance. Parents come to family therapy believing that it is impossible for them to set up such a regimen. For some families and for some patients, it *is* impossible. However, for most families of patients with early-onset, short-history anorexia nervosa, it becomes a reality.

The beginning of this revolution occurs in the second family interview, during the family picnic, when the therapist helps the parents to make their daughter eat at least one mouthful more than she wants. This symbolic act is essential, and the family meal may have to last a long time to achieve it. The parents and the patient naturally think that making the daughter eat is putting the cart before the horse. They believe that the parents' attitudes and beliefs and perhaps the patient's relationship with her family must be addressed before she can be expected to eat more than she wants. The family therapist naturally accepts that that would be the kindest and least conflictful approach, but he or she must insist that it does not happen with a reliability and predictability that can save the daughter's health and rescue her, as quickly as possible, from the hell in which she lives and might die.

The family picnic is an extremely varied occasion, as each family displays some of its feeding and mealtime rituals. Extraordinarily, most families bring a special, frugal portion for the patient and substantial quantities of food for the others. The therapist reminds them of the injunctions: "Bring enough for your daughter, who is suffering from chronic starvation. You have brought a meal for a middle-aged man, like me, on a slimming diet."

As the meal begins, the pattern of the family clearly unfolds. The therapist observes the patient's eating and begins to instruct the parents to take charge. The avoidance of confrontations and conflict that characterize the family's customary approach to dieting behavior is almost invariably apparent. The therapist suggests that the parents sit close to the patient, one on either side, and that they insist that she eat, refusing to discuss or debate how much or what she has to eat. The parents will constantly want to break away from the confrontation, to remonstrate with the therapist that success is impossible. Insistently, gently, encouragingly, the therapist presses them, in the manner that he or she wants them to compel their daughter. The therapist should frequently stand or crouch behind the parents, with his or her hands on their shoulders, urging them to be implacable, powerful, and irresistible to their daughter. Repetitive, insistent, and almost hypnotic use of suggestions by the therapist (intoning in the parents' ears) compels the parents to increase gradually the monotonous force applied to their daughter, making her eat. They may have to treat her like a toddler refusing medicine, and the therapist often uses that analogy: "Remember when she was two; if she had pneumonia and was refusing her penicillin, you would have *made* her take it." Many times, parents take this literally; one holds the patient's nose and the other pushes a sandwich into her thus forced-open mouth. The procedure is inelegant, humiliating, and inappropriate for the patient's age, but the one mouthful that the daughter eats at her parents' command and in excess of her wishes regularly marks a turning point.

The therapist needs to achieve no more during the family meal and occasionally must accept less. In many cases, the effect is striking in that the patient now knows that her parents have a new resource. Thereafter, parents often find that they can get their daughter to eat more. The struggle may be unrelenting for weeks or months, sometimes for a year or two, but parental power to enforce more food intake, if the parents put their will to it, alters the relationship among the patient, the parents, and food. The usual reaction is for the parents to gain more control, but no weight increase occurs by the next visit (occasionally very dehydrated patients will gain several kilograms). If there has been no weight gain, the therapist must begin dietary instructions—largely by eliciting from the family their large, though often unused, store of knowledge about what constitutes high-calorie foods. Many of these families are keenly aware of calorie values but have not inverted their thinking to create high-density meals. Once they have thought it through, parents become inventive, so when they fight with their daughter about a meal, the argument concerns 1,000 calories, not the negligible caloric content of fat-free yogurt, a lettuce leaf, or celery, which they had heretofore been pleased to see pass their daughter's lips.

One way in which the patient may undermine the impact of the family meal with the family therapist is to eat well. The therapist should fear such a response as a bad prognostic sign. Indeed, we find it useful to preempt such a possibility by asking the patient to resist the parents' efforts during the therapeutic family meal. We may say: "I know that you would like to be helpful because you are often upset that your parents are having such a bad time. Part of you too might be frightened that you can make them unable to stop you from starving yourself, even to death. I also guess that it is humiliating for you to be seen being made to eat. However, from my point of view, I want you to try as hard as possible to stop your parents feeding you. I don't want you to lose either your fine obstinacy or your independent spirit—not in any way. I just want you to be physically safe and to find other ways to use your strength of character and individuality." This communication has the quality of a paradoxical injunction: If the patient complies, she is doing what the therapist says he or she wants. If she does not comply, she eats at the parents' command, which is what the therapist wants. Like all useful paradoxical techniques, however, the message is also truthful. The therapist wants the patient to resist, admires her willpower, endorses her individuality and drive for independence, and wishes for her physical well-being. Other symptoms (vomiting, binging, and purging) can also be subject to strict parental control, and this control should be encouraged—specifically (as with dietary control) as a short-term measure. The intention is for the parents to demonstrate that they can achieve control and, if necessary, to remove the possibility of the patient being able to make herself ill again.

With separated parents, each set of parents should be trained to control the symptoms. The empowerment of a single parent is more difficult. A co-opted ally, friend, grandparent, or other relative can be useful, but siblings are not useful in this role. Throughout the refeeding training, the role assigned to siblings is one that does not interfere with the parents and provides uncritical support and sympathy for the patient. This is not easy to achieve and is one reason why the presence of siblings in the therapy is so strongly encouraged.

Second Phase

The first phase of treatment consists of setting up the family meetings, meeting with and engaging the family, making a family assessment, and beginning to train the family to take charge of the symptomatic behavior. The manner in which these activities have been performed has intervened in the usual patterns of family life, and change has been sought. The therapist has strongly encouraged respect for differences and acceptance of the closeness that ensues from each family member having a discrete identity.

In the second phase, the tasks of the first phase are continued with a gradual change in emphasis. After the family meal, feeding will likely be a preoccupation for one to three sessions, even when the patient is gaining weight under the new regimen. The therapist insists that the patient must have no doubt that she will not return to anorexic feeding behavior while she is part of her parents' household. The need for regular, dietetically balanced food intake is stressed; vegetarianism is temporarily disallowed; and vomiting, binging, and purging are made impossible by the closeness of parental surveillance and control. The regimen is often likened to what the parents would expect of themselves if they found that their teenager was using illicit drugs. Indeed, starvation addiction is analogous to substance addiction (Szmukler and Tantum 1984). The parents of anorexic patients (unlike the parents of young drug addicts) usually have the personal resources and family styles to develop high levels of control of their child's symptomatic behavior.

Soon in the second phase, the therapist has to press the family to relinquish control. For the first few weeks, the patient may have to be absent from school to be under parental control 24 hours a day. One or both parents may have to take leave from work, perhaps in alternation. Now the family has to reengage the outside world, with the encouragement of the therapist. The sessions become separated by 2–3 weeks and then 3–4 weeks. At the beginning of each session, the therapist weighs the patient, perhaps while talking intimately and intensely with her, asking her to be as outspoken and forceful in the family meeting as she must be to express her opinions and needs. During the session, the therapist records the patient's weight on a chart, and the graph (if it is not showing weight gain) dominates the discussion. Target weights are not strictly set. Percentile positions are used as guides for how much work must be done. The final target weight is one at which the patient ceases to worry about food and (if the patient is a girl) begins to menstruate. If the weight is not increasing, then a review of mealtime technique, food intake, and between-meal surveillance dominates the session.

In unsuccessful cases, this pattern continues for months and perhaps years. In successful cases, such discussions soon end and the family talks about problems that preoccupy most families with teenagers. This change is welcomed by the therapist, who engages in discussions about clothes, school, assignments, holiday arrangements, how late children can stay out, and so on. These discussions are serious and important because they regulate the distance and separateness of the adolescent from the parents while allowing for intimacy and closeness. Our measures of family-member self-evaluations (C. Dare, I. Eisler, and D. LeGrange, 1989, unpublished observations) using the Olson Family Adaptability Cohesion Evaluation Scales (FACES; Olson et al. 1979) have shown that members of families with anorexic patients are dissatisfied with the family, seeing the organization as too rigid and the distance between family members too great. We hypothesize that the apparent enmeshment and conflict avoidance is an attempt to counteract this dissatisfaction. The aim of therapy is to give family members additional skills and responses so that flexibility and intimate separateness replace rigidity and enmeshed distance. As yet, we are unable to demonstrate that those changes occur; clinically, however, families become more relaxed with, comfortable with, and close to each other, and there is a more open acceptance of separateness.

The second phase takes from five to seven sessions. During this phase, the patient's attitude toward the therapist will change from one of watchful, almost hostile, dependence to one that is more friendly and accepting.

The therapist's insistence that the parents prohibit the eating disorder creates a dangerous time for therapy. The family's fear, guilt, and hatred of conflict make direct confrontation seem dreadful. The simplest way for the family to avoid this confrontation is to unite and attack the therapist. The therapist has to neutralize that possibility preemptively by using great warmth and authority. If the refeeding is successful, the therapist gains prestige for a while; this prestige is used in the second phase to facilitate negotiations of the new patterns of relationships. Toward the end of the second phase, the therapist must be powerful in demoting himself or herself and empowering the parents and children to take over and respect their own rights, strengths, and skills.

Third Phase

The third phase is a brief period when the therapist and family are convinced that the symptomatic activities will no longer occur and, therefore, do not need to be discussed. The patient may still be preoccupied with food and remain worried about her shape and weight. But she is now able to talk about it in a relaxed, often puzzled way, as a persistent reminder of the nightmare from which she has escaped. Open discussion of what it has been like for her is extremely useful in convincing everyone that, despite the continuing fear that "it could all come back," a great deal has changed.

One or two sessions of discussion about the past and plans for the future are usually enough for this termination phase. The therapist has two primary tasks in these sessions:

1. To explore with the parents how much they are doing as a separate couple. How are they developing the nonparenting aspects of their lives?
2. To look at the leaving-home plans. Many families with an anorexic patient are highly committed to parenting. Indeed, it is often clear that the children have the belief that the family exists only to look after themselves. A corollary to this is the belief that the parents' marriage has no real dynamic power as a love relationship. This may secretly or overtly be the view of the parents, but it may be only a fantasy in the children's minds. Either way, in the terminating sessions, the therapist works hard to help the parents learn that they can take care of themselves, that they can seek their own path as separate individuals and as a couple, and that they do not need children as a reason for existence. Many families with anorexic patients seem to believe the myth that the patient's illness has provided the parents with a sick child who will never grow up and will, therefore, keep the mother and father together

as parents whereas otherwise they would have nothing in common. The parents have sometimes perpetuated this myth by saying: "We live for our children." This is admirable, but the therapist must ask, "What are you going to live for when the children look after themselves?"

The aim of the ending session is not to resolve these matters; it is to get the parents to make it clear to the children that these matters are the parents' business (not the children's) and that they will attend to them.

Conclusion

We have described a form of family therapy that has had a high level of success. But there are failures. For example, families may be unable to face refeeding. This is unusual, but it has happened, especially if an additional family crisis has occurred (e.g., the death of a grandparent). More often, the failure is in the second phase. The family never establishes a parent-controlled weight gain in the patient. She herself allows a gain of a few kilograms and the crisis of acute starvation is over, but the problem is never confronted. Sometimes the parents do achieve some control, but the weight is insufficient to return the daughter to good health and she remains chronically anorexic. Obviously, we then extend the treatment and try various family therapy techniques. We also use individual meetings with the patient to attempt to establish a more effective therapeutic alliance with her. This alliance can be established, but it is not a guarantee that the treatment will evolve successfully. Some of the failed cases are associated with obvious marital problems, and we have attempted marital therapy to reduce the conflict and disharmony that interfere with being effective parents. This strategy may be successful for the marriage, but its benefits for the patient may be limited.

We have evidence that very low initial weight, higher levels of critical comments, and high levels of self-reported dissatisfaction with family life predict a poor outcome for family therapy (Dare et al. 1990). In principle, we should be able to devise techniques to counter the level of critical comments, using the methods shown to be effective with families containing a schizophrenic patient (Leff and Vaughn 1985). In practice, we have not shown that we can do this. We do know that many families report that they are happier with family life (Nitz 1987; H. Nitz and C. Dare, 1984, unpublished observations), but we do not know if we can achieve this in the worst cases.

References

Blitzer JR, Rollings N, Blackwell A: Children who starve themselves: anorexia nervosa. Psychosom Med 23:369–383, 1961

Bruch H: Eating Disorder. London, Routledge & Kegan Paul, 1974

Byng-Hall J: Family myths used as defence in conjoint family therapy. Br J Med Psychol 46:239–249, 1973

Byng-Hall J: Re-editing family mythology during family therapy. Journal of Marital and Family Therapy 1:103–116, 1979

Charcot JM: Diseases of the Nervous System, Vol 3. London, New Sydenham Society, 1889

Dare C: Family therapy for families containing an anorectic youngster, in Understanding Anorexia Nervosa and Bulimia: Report of the Fourth Ross Conference on Medical Research. Columbus, OH, Ross Laboratories, 1983, pp 28–34

Dare C: The family therapy of anorexia nervosa. J Psychiatr Res 19:435–443, 1985

Dare C: Psychoanalytic family therapy, in Family Therapy in Britain. Edited by Street E, Dryden W. New York, Open University Press, 1988, pp 23–50

Dare C, Eisler I, Russell GFM, et al: Family therapy for anorexia nervosa: implications from the results of a controlled trial of family and individual therapy. Journal of Marital and Family Therapy (in press)

Gull WW: Anorexia nervosa (apepsia hysterica, anorexia hysterica) (1874), in Evolution of Psychosomatic Concepts, Anorexia Nervosa: A Paradigm. Edited by Kaufman MR, Heiman M. New York, International Universities Press, 1964, pp 132–138

Haley J: Problem-Solving Therapy. San Francisco, CA, Jossey-Bass, 1976

Haley J: Leaving Home. New York, McGraw-Hill, 1980

Kog E, Vandereycken W, Vertommen H: The psychosomatic family model: a critical analysis of family interaction concepts. Journal of Marital and Family Therapy 7:31–44, 1985

Lasègue EC: On hysterical anorexia (1873), in Evolution of Psychosomatic Concepts, Anorexia Nervosa: A Paradigm. Edited by Kaufman MR, Heiman M. New York, International Universities Press, 1964, pp 141–155

Leff J, Vaughn C: Expressed Emotion in Families. New York, Guilford, 1985

Lorand S: Anorexia nervosa: a report of a case (1943), in Evolution of Psychosomatic Concepts, Anorexia Nervosa: A Paradigm. Edited by Kaufman MR, Heiman M. New York, International Universities Press, 1964, pp 298–319

Madanes C: Strategic Family Therapy. New York, Jossey-Bass, 1981

Martin FE: The treatment and outcome of anorexia nervosa in adolescence: a prospective study and five year follow-up. J Psychiatr Res 19:509–514, 1985

Masserman JH: Psychodynamics in anorexia nervosa and neurotic vomiting (1941), in Evolution of Psychosomatic Concepts, Anorexia Nervosa: A Paradigm. Edited by Kaufman MR, Heiman M. New York, International Universities Press, 1964, pp 320–351

Minuchin S: Psychoanalytic therapies and the low socioeconomic population, in Modern Psychoanalysis. Edited by Marmor J. New York, Basic Books, 1970, pp 532–550

Minuchin S, Baker L, Rosman BL, et al: A conceptual model of psychosomatic illness in children: family organization and family therapy. Arch Gen Psychiatry 32:1031–1038, 1975

Minuchin S, Rosman BL, Baker L: Psychosomatic Families. Cambridge, MA, Harvard University Press, 1978

Nitz H: Anorexia Nervosa bei Jugendlichen. Berlin, Springer-Verlag, 1987

Olson DH, Sprenkle DH, Russell CS: Circumplex-model of marital and family systems, I: cohesion and adaptability dimensions, family types and clinical application. Fam Process 18:3–28, 1979

Rotrok C, Wllisch D, Schroder J: A family therapy outcome study in an inpatient setting. Am J Orthopsychiatry 47: 514–522, 1977

Russell GFM, Szmukler GI, Eisler I, et al: An evaluation of family therapy in anorexia nervosa and bulimia nervosa. Arch Gen Psychiatry 44:265–271, 1987

Ryle JA: Anorexia nervosa. Lancet 2:893–899, 1936

Sargent J, Liebman R, Silver M: Family therapy for anorexia nervosa, in Handbook of Psychotherapy for Anorexia Nervosa and Bulimia Nervosa. Edited by Garner DM, Garfinkel PE. London, Guilford, 1985

Selvini-Palazzoli M: Self-starvation. London, Human Context, 1974

Stanton MD: Strategic approaches to family therapy, in Handbook of Family Therapy. Edited by Gurman AS, Kniskern DP. New York, Brunner/Mazel, 1981, pp 361–402

Stern S, Whitaker CA, Hagemann NJ, et al: Anorexia nervosa: the hospital's role in treatment. Fam Process 30:395–408, 1981

Szmukler GI, Tantum T: Anorexia nervosa: starvation dependence. Br J Med Psychol 57:303–310, 1984

Szmukler GI, Eisler I, Dare C: Systematic observation and clinical insight: are they compatible? an experiment recognizing family interaction. Psychol Med 15:701–737, 1985a

Szmukler GI, Eisler I, Russell GFM, et al: Anorexia nervosa, parental "expressed emotion" and dropping out of treatment. Br J Psychiatry 147:265–271, 1985b

Szmukler GI, Berkowitz R, Eisler I, et al: A comparative study of parental "expressed emotion" in individual and family settings. Br J Psychiatry 151:174–178, 1987

Thoma H: Anorexia Nervosa. New York, International Universities Press, 1967

Waller JV, Kaufman MR, Deutsh F: Anorexia nervosa: a psychosomatic entity (1940), in Evolution of Psychosomatic Concepts, Anorexia Nervosa: A Paradigm. Edited by Kaufman MR, Heiman M. New York, International Universities Press, 1964, pp 245–273

White M: Anorexia nervosa: a transgenerational perspective. Fam Process 22:255–273, 1983

Wynne LC: Paradoxical interventions: leverage for therapeutic change in individuals and family systems, in The Psychotherapy of Schizophrenia. Edited by Strauss JS, Bowers M, Downey WT, et al. New York, Plenum, 1980, pp 191–202

Yager J: Family issues in the pathogenesis of anorexia nervosa. Psychosom Med 44:43–60, 1982

Chapter 3

Outpatient Family Therapy for Bulimia Nervosa

JACK S. BRANDES, M.D., Ph.D., F.R.C.P.(C)

Chapter 3

Outpatient Family Therapy for Bulimia Nervosa

*T*reatment of bulimia nervosa (BN) with outpatient family therapy is still in an early phase of development. This situation also applies to other therapies for BN, such as individual systemic (Root et al. 1986), individual cognitive-behavioral (Fairburn 1985; Wilson 1986), group (Mitchell et al. 1985; Yager 1985), pharmacotherapy (Wilson 1986), or combined therapies (Johnson and Pure 1986; Wooley and Kearney-Cooke 1986; Wooley and Wooley 1985; Yager 1985), because only recently has this eating disorder been differentiated from anorexia nervosa (AN) (Garfinkel et al. 1980; Johnson et al. 1984; Russell 1979). The few reports describing family treatment for BN are theoretical (Humphrey and Stern 1988; Madanes 1981; Roberto 1986; Root et al. 1986; Schwartz et al. 1985; Selvini-Palazzoli and Viaro 1988). The only empirical assessment of the efficacy of family therapy for BN suggests that when it is used without other forms of intervention, this modality alone is not sufficient (Russell et al. 1987).

In spite of the somewhat unexplored nature of BN and the sparse guidance for clinicians, bulimic individuals and their families turn to us for help. In this chapter I review some of the treatments that have been suggested for use with BN families, suggest a novel framework based on my clinical experience, and examine some of the clinical problems and issues facing family therapists dealing with bulimic patients in private practice or a clinical setting.

Family Typologies: A Brief Review

There have been several attempts to describe the bulimic patient's family system to understand the relational context in which symptoms appear and to develop therapeutic approaches to the bulimia. Current descriptions of BN families may bear some similarities to earlier or current descriptions of AN families (Schwartz et al. 1985). That there are similarities is not surprising because 50% of patients with BN have a prior history of AN (Garfinkel et al. 1980), but the significance of these similarities remains to be investigated.

Minuchin (1974) and Minuchin et al. (1978) focused on interactional behavior seen during family therapy sessions and described five patterns typical in psychosomatic families: enmeshment, overprotectiveness, rigidity, lack of ability to resolve conflicts, and involvement of the patient in parental conflict. Schwartz et al. (1985) agreed that these behavioral patterns are applicable to BN families, and they added several other characteristic features, including social isolation, consciousness of appearance, and attaching special meaning to food and eating. These features, unlike those in the list developed by Minuchin, are descriptive of family attitudes and behavior that may not be observable in therapy sessions but can be elicited when taking a history.

Schwartz et al. (1985) used somewhat global social descriptors to classify BN families into three broad groups: "all-American" families, ethnic families, and mixed families. Each group's descriptor is based on how the family relates to its understanding of its internal legacy and its understanding of the external demands of society. Schwartz et al. (1985) suggested that all BN families are extraordinarily concerned with values and ideals, whether originating outside the family system, as in the all-American family, or inside the system, as in the ethnic family. Furthermore, these values and ideals seem to supersede any individual's need, wish, capacity, or (in extreme situations) personhood. They suggest that these families' attitudes of selflessness and sacrifice to group values and ideals is mediated through the unresolved loss of a stable, nurturing "kinship network" that the family no longer has available and that the family's consequent attempt to replace the loss leads to its rigid attitudinal position. The search for security and connectedness allows the family to fall prey to the primacy of the value of self-sacrifice to external social fashion or internal loyalty demands despite this value's nature being inimical to personal growth and development.

Selvini-Palazzoli (1978) and Selvini-Palazzoli and Viaro (1988), who clearly noted the tendency for self-sacrifice in families of patients with eating disorders, also pointed out the absence of clear leadership in these family systems. The families apparently have no one in charge. These observations complement those of Schwartz et al. (1985) and Minuchin's focus on enmeshment, overprotectiveness, and defective conflict resolution in these family systems. The following comments from BN patients and their families (for whom I have provided care) echo these issues; they describe their lack of empowerment to be and to grow, their lack of entitlement to make demands on others, and their lack of control over what is expected by others.

Miss A: The central issue in my life is that . . . I don't exist, I'm screaming at the top of my lungs, and there is no response . . . not even a ripple.
Miss B: I'm the American ideal . . . I'm dead.
Miss A's father: Our relationship won't change much . . . she [his wife] can't see me as someone with needs.
Miss C: Everyone expects things of me . . . I want to do things to shock them into reality that I'm human.

Kog and Vandereycken (1985) reviewed the research literature on the family characteristics of families with anorexic and bulimic patients. They noted that the recurrent findings include controlling interdependent family relationships, parental discord, and a high incidence of physical illness, affective disorder, and alcoholism in the extended family. These findings, based on a series of population studies the authors reviewed, parallel the more descriptive theoretical work already mentioned. A small series study from France (Igoin-Apfelbaum 1985) of 21 bulimic women also describes histories of separation and loss with consequent enmeshment and isolation of families.

Root et al. (1986) proposed another framework for family typology in BN. Their contribution, which is based on a systemic and feminist approach to BN, is the most detailed and comprehensive now available. The family types they described are the perfect family, the overprotective family, and the chaotic family. This typology is global and bears an interesting resemblance to the three categories of Schwartz et al. (1985). The parallels between the all-American and the perfect family, the overprotective and the ethnic family, and the mixed and the chaotic family are striking. Both systems of classification agree that all families with bulimic patients have individual and subsystem boundary problems; that weight, appearance, competence, and achievement are important factors; and that the development of BN reflects a systemic difficulty in the negotiation of the transition from adolescence to young adulthood and independence for the children and parents in BN families.

These descriptive typologies are useful in helping a clinician recognize the family with which he or she is working, but they are not anchored in an explanatory framework, a sort of "pathophysiology." This state of affairs produces much confusion for therapists and researchers (Schwartz et al. 1985). The absence of an explanatory framework leads to univariate theories of etiology and treatment of laundry lists of symptoms and maladaptive behavior patterns to be handled. The next section highlights some of the common observations regarding bulimic patients and their families that suggest an explanatory framework that might be of value for practicing clinicians and researchers.

Attachment and Loss Dynamics and Bulimia Nervosa

The difficulty that bulimic patients and their families have in dealing with normal growth and maturation has been noted. Their sense of isolation or disconnection from an extended family or society at large has also been described. Clinical observation suggests that their valiant attempts to deal with this unpleasant state of affairs include adopting external social or internal family values regardless of the damage these values cause (Schwartz et al. 1985). The collective selves in the family tend to be sacrificed to values and ideals that bear little relation to the actual biological and psychological needs of each individual in these families. Could this rigid, self-destructive patterning represent the means, maladaptive as it is, for coping with isolation, separation, and loss? Interpersonal enmeshment and overprotectiveness, deficits in conflict resolution, lack of leadership, and difficulty in assisting children to mature all point in this direction. Furthermore, families of bulimic patients often give histories of actual loss and abandonment through the illness and death of an important family member, change in socioeconomic status, or immigration and subsequent social isolation.

Bowlby (1982, 1984) suggested that unresolved loss or separation leads to the development of a chronic protest or detached behavior pattern rather than to resolution through normal grieving or mourning. Protest behavior includes anger, irritability, object seeking (including food and drugs), hyperactivity, and emotionality. Detachment patterns include coolness, object withdrawal, emotional distancing, and rationalization. When a mourning process (which seems to require a group-supported affective experience) is unavailable to an individual or a family to allow for the resolution of loss, the abandoned individual or family can oscillate between these two states of protest and detachment when attempting to deal with further losses or separations. Caretaking and parenting in families dealing with unresolved loss and isolation become more difficult as the shifting demands of normal growth and maturation produce a continual series of losses and activate these patterns. For example, a child's normal shift in interest from a parent to a peer group could be experienced as a painful and hurtful act by an isolated, lonely parent. Perfect families behave in a manner that suggests a detachment pattern of functioning:

> We seem to be having a small problem with our daughter, if you say so, doctor. . . . I suppose vomiting several times a day could be normal in the broadest sense. Wasn't it done in some cultures? . . . Aside from this matter, nothing much is out of order.

The predominant pattern of overprotective families parallels the object-seeking behavior of the protest phase:

> How dare she upset us this way? What a lack of gratitude for all we have done for her, for all the sacrifices. . . . We are so concerned and hurt by this terrible vomiting, I can't sleep thinking about it . . . she may die . . . you must save her, doctor . . . I am furious at her.

Figure 1 displays the dynamics of attachment and loss.

A further behavioral aspect of families with bulimic patients suggests that the system has difficulty with attachment and loss. The concern with physical appearance, deportment, performance, and demeanor is highly exaggerated in these families and, in all probability, represents an excessive concern about the shame of appearing unappealing and unacceptable to society. Lewis (1987) suggested that shame is a central affective response to the internal perception of incipient loss or abandonment and is crucial for regulating attachments. Shame of being too fat is a recurring theme in our society, particularly for women (Silberstein et al. 1987), and

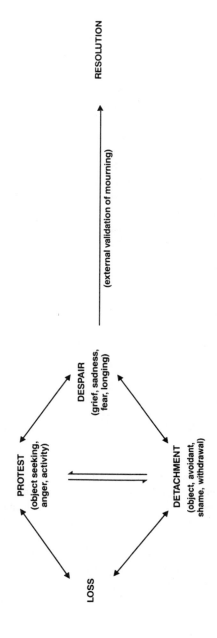

FIGURE 1. Dynamics of attachment and loss.

it is a dominant concern for bulimic individuals and their families. Furthermore, shame and embarrassment about the self and the family are easily noted in the dialogue of family or individual sessions and in the tendency toward secretiveness seen in bulimic patients and their families.

Miss A: If I feel I look well, there are possibilities in the world; if not, there are none and I don't feel loved inside.

Miss A's father: We pull apart over stress because we have to be perfect all the time . . . everyone in this family is a source of shame. . . . My problem is that I can't tell her no right there; I'm too embarrassed . . . so she doesn't see me as a person . . . I withdraw.

Miss C: Failure is a sign of shame and badness . . . you feel rejected.

Miss D: If I make a fool of myself in a relationship, the only way I can go meet someone else is if I spend two repentant days in bed suffering for my stupidity. (Garfinkel and Garner 1982, p. 299)

When a clinician can conceptualize the family dynamics of the bulimic system in terms of its compromised regulation of the inevitable sequelae of loss as the result of unresolved loss and isolation, the confusion of descriptive typologies currently in use can be avoided and a coherent therapeutic stance can emerge. A therapist's (or therapeutic team's) position must allow for the family system's access to the therapist regardless of whether the family is immediately involved in treatment, address the difficulty that the system faces when dealing with change or loss, and avoid the stimulation of further shame or loss for the family. The patient's maturational retardation can then be framed in terms of her concern for preventing loss for and shame to her family of origin.

This framework does not deal with the problem of symptom choice. Why is the fear of maturation and development (separation or loss and shame) focused on body size and weight regulation? Could this reflect a family's perception of an important external social value that, if adopted by the identified patient, would allow the family to be accepted and reconnected with society at large? Such a hypothesis might partially explain the rapid increase in the incidence of BN during the past two decades. What aspect of the patient's dynamics and attachment pattern make her vulnerable to accepting this task from her family?

Therapeutic Issues

Clinical Presentation and Early Stages of Treatment

Although BN seems to be a relatively common condition in our society, only a small percentage of individuals suffering from it seek treatment (Fairburn and Cooper 1983; Pyle et al. 1983). This finding is consistent with the clinical observation that bulimic patients are often brought to therapy by their families or seek psychiatric treatment for problems other than just the bulimia. Having decided to seek treatment, bulimic individuals may find it difficult to divulge the extent and pervasiveness of their symptomatology. The bulimic patient's secrecy has been commented on (Herzog 1982) and is an expression of the tremendous shame of these individuals and their families. Needless to say, this tendency to hide and obscure makes assessment difficult (Johnson and Pure 1986). A clinician can easily be induced by a bulimic patient and her family system to overlook areas of inquiry and proceed with a treatment plan without all of the facts. Unless specifically asked about areas such as change in family socioeconomic status, abuse, addictions, and psychiatric illness, family members will rarely offer this information and often downplay it. The use of checklists when beginning with a new patient may prevent this countertransference to the patient's shame and provide the clinician with valuable material for the therapeutic work ahead.

The clinician must also take the referral route into account when beginning the assessment of a bulimic patient. Often, the patient is not the person seeking treatment for her problem. Her family of origin, spouse, or physician might be forcing her to deal with the bulimia. This issue is best addressed by asking the patient and family directly. When the request for treatment is not made by the patient, attention to the referring family or system member is important to prevent scapegoating and to help the bulimic individual "own" her bulimia (Selvini-Palazzoli et al. 1980). This is echoed in the words of Patient A: "I'm a burden to someone by the fact that I exist. I want so badly to define my own reality . . . not other peoples'."

The clinician's most useful stance in dealing with the family and the individual, regardless of the mode of referral, was best described by Boszormenyi-Nagy and Krasner (1986) as "multidirected partiality." This involves a willingness to experience concern and care for all members of the bulimic patient's family so that inadvertent scapegoating of parents, siblings, spouses, children, and the patient does not occur during assessment and treatment. Bulimic symptoms may play a central role in the life of the patient's family. Their persistence can induce guilt, shame, frustration, helplessness, desperation, and anger in all who deal with them. The illness often symbolizes the relational bind in which the family and the bulimic patient live.

> Miss A: I'm starving to death and things are being forced down my throat; I lack the entitlement to get good food—to not swallow the shit—that's why I vomit it up. I have to live like this—the way they require it.
>
> Miss A's mother: We live a legacy that destroys us. My mother will never recognize me. I couldn't claim a place either.

Ideally, all members of a bulimic patient's family should be seen so that the clinician can formulate a clear picture of the family dynamics and decide on an appropriate treatment. Excluding available family members from the assessment process can seriously hinder the therapy (Boszormenyi-Nagy 1972; Boszormenyi-Nagy and Spark 1973). The inclusion of family members may simply involve several exploratory sessions during the assessment phase of treatment or, if indicated, concurrent family therapy for the whole family and marital therapy for the patient's parents or for the patient and her spouse. The choice of therapeutic approach will depend on the nature of the family system and its availability and motivation to undertake therapeutic work. The therapist must remain available to the family regardless of whether the family decides to become involved in treatment at the outset.

The clinician's partiality should extend to the physical as well as the psychological aspects of the bulimic patient's health. Bulimic behavior carries significant risk to the patient's body and must be monitored and handled by the clinician or a medical colleague, preferably not the family therapist. Finally, the family therapist must be willing to share the therapeutic burden with other health care professionals. Individual therapy, group therapy, pharmacotherapy, dietary education, and hospitalization

Table 1. Components of assessment for outpatient family therapy of bulimia nervosa

1. Family interview
2. Individual interview with patient
3. Interview with patient's parents
4. Medical and dental assessment
5. Psychological testing of patient and family: defensive styles, ability to cope with loss, and affective lability

may all be required during treatment. Table 1 presents the components of an outpatient assessment for bulimia nervosa.

Some Treatment Problems

At the outset of work with the family of a bulimic patient, two difficult matters must be addressed. 1) The patient's accessibility for treatment requires simultaneous assessment of and attention to the starvation and physiological sequelae of her binge-purge behavior. 2) The bulimic patient must join with her bulimic family to allow for development of a functional treatment relationship.

The cognitive and behavioral effects of starvation can produce signs and symptoms of psychiatric illness, medical illness, and personality disorders and render the patient inaccessible to treatment (Kaplan and Woodside 1987). Refeeding and attention to endocrine and electrolyte imbalances must precede psychotherapeutic work. At best, supportive interventions are useful until this has been achieved.

Coercion by the family or spouse or secretly sought treatment by the bulimic patient sets up a complicating, guilt-inducing dynamic that impedes development of a treatment alliance and produces a therapeutic bind in which either the patient or the family is "bad" (Selvini-Palazzoli 1982). The therapist's stance of multidirected partiality is useful here. Both the family's coerciveness and the patient's secretiveness protect the family's integrity; as such, they should be addressed in a way that allows the system to remain shame-free and whole. The bulimic patient's physical integrity can also be addressed in the same way. Neither she nor her symptoms can be seen as bad, but their sequelae must be dealt with so that the psychological treatment process can begin.

Before undertaking the assessment of a patient with BN and her family system, it would be wise for the clinician to take stock of his or her own treatment support system. Bulimic patients and their families often require help in many problem areas, including affective disorder, drug and alcohol addiction, general health, parenting skills, and integration into the community at large. The clinician ought to have good access to medical and dental facilities to help in the assessment and treatment of the biological sequelae of the bulimia (hypokalemia, gastric irritation, bowel dysfunction, dental caries) and to psychiatric facilities that can provide hospitalization or day hospital programs when required during treatment. Family therapy is but one part of an integrated treatment program

(Garfinkel and Garner 1982; Root et al. 1986). Individual and group therapy, dietary education, assertiveness training, and specific attention to the sequelae of abuse may all be required in any given case. Therefore, the family therapist must develop a collaborative treatment system with colleagues who can provide these modalities as they prove necessary. See Table 2 for a list of resources for outpatient family therapy.

A further useful element in the therapist's treatment support system is a supervisory consultant. Bulimic patients and their families present the therapist with many opportunities to experience strong countertransference feelings. The difficulties that these families have with shame, attachment and loss, aggression, fear, and self-sacrifice can tax the skills and capacities of even the most experienced therapists. An external consultant can be invaluable in helping the clinician move out of an enmeshed (overattached) position or deal with the constant projection of fear, distrust, and anger that accompanies the exploration of the family's and patient's lives.

When the bulimic patient and her family see the onset of treatment as having the potential for inducing shame or the destruction of the family, powerful countertherapeutic forces are mobilized even as the initial consultation is requested. It is useful for the clinician to identify these feelings early and reassure everyone that he or she is partial to their individual struggles and the family's survival. Shame must be dealt with openly when there is evidence of it during interaction. The patient's symptoms and the family's mode of functioning must be accepted and demystified as the assessment progresses. A psychoeducational approach is exceedingly valuable in reducing the mystery of psychiatric help and can reframe much of the patient's symptomatology and the family's dy-

Table 2. Resources for outpatient family therapy of bulimia nervosa

1. Medical consultant: general medicine, gynecology, endocrinology
2. Dental consultant
3. Psychiatric inpatient service
4. Psychiatric day hospital
5. Nutritional counseling
6. Specific treatment areas (if necessary): addiction, abuse
7. Other psychological treatments: group therapy
8. Family therapy consultant for the therapist or therapy team
9. Self-help and support groups

namics in terms of growth and learning problems as opposed to "shameful" characteristics and deviations.

The major thrust of family intervention in the early stages of treatment is to reduce the sense of shame in the system, to support the family when it is concerned about familial disintegration, and to reactivate the normal maturational process in the system. (See Table 3 for the stages of outpatient family therapy.) The symptom of bulimia is best dealt with when it becomes the sole property of the bulimic individual. Whether the bulimic patient is a spouse or a child, the clear-cut ownership of the symptom helps to undo the interlocking guilt, anger, shame, and overinvolvement in the system. It is helpful for the clinician to review with everyone how they will feel when only the bulimic patient has to deal with her symptoms after indicating that the bulimia belongs only to the symptomatic family member. Sessions in which the family and the bulimic patient separately review the same material about the effects of the binge-purge cycle help establish this separateness.

The early family sessions are also used to deal with feelings relating to treatment and its goals, course, and ramifications for the system. The

Table 3.   Stages of outpatient family therapy of bulimia nervosa

Assessment phase
   Joining with family and patient
   History
   Evaluating route of referral
   Addressing shame and blame in system
   Education—biology and psychology of bulimia nervosa

Early treatment phase
   Contract with family and individual for treatment
   Ownership of bulimia
   Dietary reeducation
   Loss and abandonment theme in family
   Self-sacrifice and individual identity in family

Middle treatment phase
   Individual concerns—femininity, identity
   Marital issues
   Separation in family
   Integration into community

Termination
   Focus on loss and abandonment in the treatment
   Contract for future contacts with therapist

potential for growth and development is not always a positive experience for frightened, rigid families that fear loss, abandonment, and shame. The clinician's clarity and straightforwardness will assist the family and the bulimic patient to develop confidence in the treatment. It is also reassuring for the bulimic individual and her family to know that the therapist has a thorough understanding of the bulimic syndrome in terms of physical and psychological sequelae. When the therapist shares this information, it does much to develop a mutual sense of trust and purpose.

The clinician must be alert to and prepared to handle specific treatment problems, including the medical sequelae of starvation, vomiting, and laxative abuse; the use of street drugs and alcohol; suicide risk; depression; and ongoing sexual abuse. These are not matters that can be handled late in the treatment. The decision to work exclusively with the family, individually with the bulimic patient, or in a group with concurrent family sessions can only be made after the assessment is complete. It is likely that family or couple sessions will have to be supplemented with individual work to deal with matters such as sexuality and abuse. Self-help groups can play a role late in the treatment when a working treatment alliance with the therapist is established. Some bulimic patients experience these groups as a useful adjunct to the individual and family work and as a means of becoming less isolated.

As mentioned before, bulimic individuals and their families find loss and separation difficult. Their sense of isolation and vulnerability to shame make it difficult for these systems to be open to and accepting of external input. This accounts for the obstacles the patients face in negotiating the shifts from childhood to adolescence and from adolescence to adulthood. Once the family is well engaged in treatment, the difficulty in dealing with loss and change can be addressed. Both concrete structural approaches and cognitive and psychoeducational techniques can be used to acquaint the family with the range of reaction to loss. The family's evoked memory of actual loss experiences is often extremely useful in exploring this area and allows the clinician to assess the manner in which these experiences are handled by each family member. Death, illness, and physical separation (such as going away to school and camp) often provide graphic ongoing examples for the family. Memories of more distant experiences such as sad movies and incidents that have impinged less directly on the family may be the only material available when families are particularly vulnerable. The clinician must remain sensitive to the actual capacity the family has to mourn when experiencing a loss and must not force the system to experience more sadness than it can handle.

Normal sadness and mourning cannot be accessed by the family or the individual unless there is an understanding that there will be a support system available to them when the process emerges. Often, these families, as a result of their isolation, have not had the opportunity to internalize the sense of a consoling, comforting other to empower them to feel and express their grief and sadness. Thus, loss triggers effects that must be strangled and suppressed, leaving the family and its members in an oscillating protest or detached pattern, unable to "metabolize" the loss and unable to cope with change and growth within themselves and their system.

Bulimic patients and their families also have difficulty finishing therapy (Igoin-Apfelbaum 1985). Growth and change produce loss and its attendant shame, sadness, and disconnection. The clinician must be aware of this from the outset and realize that his or her connection with the family system may be more prolonged than anticipated. The use of multiple therapist contacts in working with these families helps somewhat, but the family must be encouraged to become involved in community, religious, and social activities that promote growth and development outside the therapeutic system.

Summary

The treatment of BN with outpatient family therapy continues to develop and change as we understand more about the basic dynamic, social, and physiological aspects of this condition. This chapter reviews some of the literature on outpatient family treatment of bulimia and suggests an approach to this condition by understanding the dynamics of separation and loss. The framework suggested may prove useful to organize further research into the underlying psychological and physiological mechanisms of BN and to provide a coherent therapeutic approach to this condition.

References

Boszormenyi-Nagy I: Loyalty implications of the transference model in psychotherapy. Arch Gen Psychiatry 27: 374–380, 1972

Boszormenyi-Nagy I, Krasner B: Between Give and Take: A Clinical Guide to Contextual Therapy. New York, Brunner/Mazel, 1986

Boszormenyi-Nagy I, Spark G: Invisible Loyalties: Reciprocity in Intergenerational Family Therapy. New York, Harper & Row, 1973

Bowlby J: Attachment and loss: retrospect and prospect. Am J Orthopsychiatry 52:664–678, 1982

Bowlby J: Violence in the family as a disorder of the attachment and caregiving systems. Am J Psychoanal 44:9–27, 1984

Fairburn CG: Cognitive-behavioral treatment for bulimia, in Handbook of Psychotherapy for Anorexia Nervosa and Bulimia. Edited by Garner DM, Garfinkel PE. New York, Guilford, 1985, pp 160–192

Fairburn CG, Cooper PJ: The epidemiology of bulimia nervosa: two community studies. International Journal of Eating Disorders 2:61–67, 1983

Garfinkel PE, Garner DM: Anorexia Nervosa: A Multidimensional Perspective. New York, Brunner/Mazel, 1982

Garfinkel PE, Moldofsky H, Garner DM: The heterogeneity of anorexia nervosa: bulimia as a distinct subgroup. Arch Gen Psychiatry 37:1036–1040, 1980

Herzog DB: Bulimia: the secretive syndrome. Psychosomatics 23:481–487, 1982

Humphrey LL, Stern S: Object relations and the family system in bulimia: a theoretical integration. Journal of Marital and Family Therapy 14:337–350, 1988

Igoin-Apfelbaum L: Characteristics of family background in bulimia. Psychother Psychosom 43:161–167, 1985

Johnson C, Pure DL: Assessment of bulimia: a multidimensional model, in Handbook of Eating Disorders. Edited by Brownell KD, Foreyt JP. New York, Basic Books, 1986, pp 405–449

Johnson C, Lewis C, Hagman J: The syndrome of bulimia: review and synthesis. Psychiatr Clin North Am 7:247–273, 1984

Kaplan AS, Woodside DB: Biological aspects of anorexia nervosa and bulimia nervosa. J Consult Clin Psychol 55: 645–653, 1987

Kog E, Vandereycken W: Family characteristics of anorexia nervosa and bulimia: a review of the research literature. Clin Psychol Rev 5:159–180, 1985

Lewis HB: The role of shame in depression over the life span, in The Role of Shame in Symptom Formation. Edited by Lewis HB. Hillsdale, NJ, Lawrence Erlbaum, 1987, pp 29–50

Madanes C: Strategic Family Therapy. San Francisco, CA, Jossey-Bass, 1981

Minuchin S: Families and Family Therapy. Cambridge, MA, Harvard University Press, 1974

Minuchin S, Rosman B, Baker L: Psychosomatic Families: Anorexia Nervosa in Context. Cambridge, MA, Harvard University Press, 1978

Mitchell JE, Hatsukami D, Goff G, et al: Intensive outpatient group treatment for bulimia, in Handbook of Psychotherapy for Anorexia Nervosa and Bulimia. Edited by Garner DM, Garfinkel PE. New York, Guilford, 1985, pp 240–256

Pyle RL, Mitchell JE, Eckert ED, et al: The incidence of bulimia in freshman college students. International Journal of Eating Disorders 2:75–85, 1983

Roberto L: Bulimia: the transgenerational view. Journal of Marital and Family Therapy 12:231–240, 1986

Root MPP, Fallon P, Friedrich WN: Bulimia: A Systems Approach to Treatment. New York, WW Norton, 1986

Russell GM: Bulimia nervosa: an ominous variant of anorexia nervosa. Psychol Med 9:429–448, 1979

Russell GM, Szmukler GI, Dare C, et al: An evaluation of family therapy in anorexia nervosa and bulimia nervosa. Arch Gen Psychiatry 44:1047–1056, 1987

Schwartz RC, Barrett MJ, Saba G: Family therapy for bulimia, in Handbook of Psychotherapy for Anorexia Nervosa and Bulimia. Edited by Garner DM, Garfinkel PE. New York, Guilford, 1985, pp 280–310

Selvini-Palazzoli M: Self Starvation: From Individual to Family Therapy in the Treatment of Anorexia Nervosa. New York, Jason Aronson, 1978

Selvini-Palazzoli M: Snares in family therapy. Journal of Marital and Family Therapy 8:443–450, 1982

Selvini-Palazzoli M, Viaro M: The anorectic process in the family: a six-stage model as a guide for individual therapy. Fam Process 27:129–148, 1988

Selvini-Palazzoli M, Boscolo L, Cecchin GF, et al: The problem of the referring person. Journal of Marital and Family Therapy 6:3–9, 1980

Silberstein LR, Striegel-Moore R, Rodin J: Feeling fat: a woman's shame, in The Role of Shame in Symptom Formation. Edited by Lewis HB. Hillsdale, NJ, Lawrence Erlbaum, 1987, pp 89–108

Wilson GI: Cognitive-behavioral and pharmacological therapies for bulimia, in Handbook of Eating Disorders. Edited by Brownell KD, Foreyt JP. New York, Basic Books, 1986, pp 450–475

Wooley SC, Kearney-Cooke A: Intensive treatment of body-image disturbance, in Handbook of Eating Disorders. Edited by Brownell KD, Foreyt JP. New York, Basic Books, 1986, pp 476–502

Wooley SC, Wooley OW: Intensive outpatient and residential treatment for bulimia, in Handbook of Psychotherapy for Anorexia Nervosa and Bulimia. Edited by Garner DM, Garfinkel PE. New York, Guilford, 1985

Yager J: The outpatient treatment of bulimia. Bull Menninger Clin 49:203–226, 1985

Chapter 4

Impasses in the Family Treatment of Bulimia

LAURA GIAT ROBERTO, Psy.D.

Chapter 4

Impasses in the Family Treatment of Bulimia

*B*ulimia nervosa (BN) is a symptom cluster that can carry chronic emotional consequences, including depression, generalized anxiety, difficulties with intimacy, and deficits in the ability to tolerate conflict (Roberto 1987; Root et al. 1986). Physiologically, severe medical dysfunctions can result from self-induced purging, some of which can be life threatening, such as electrolyte disturbance (potassium and chloride depletion) and dehydration (Russell 1979). The high-risk nature of treating BN, in patients above or below normal weight, predisposes the therapeutic treatment team to take an active, directive stance that will prevent crisis and sustain life. Yet, regardless of the treatment model used—behavioral, object relations, or systemic—treating BN appears to engender specific therapeutic impasses that make the process of change difficult and the potential for relapse high. Because BN is primarily a disorder of adolescence, the "second individuation" and launching stage of the family life-cycle, it is perhaps inevitable that such a challenging and active psychotherapy should produce intense reactions in the participants. From a systemic viewpoint, however, patterns of organization in marriages and families with bulimic individuals interact with characteristics of the treatment team or therapist to create specific management problems (or impasses) that can impede and prevent change. In this chapter, I review interpersonal patterns in spouses and families of bulimic patients, which have been identified at the Center for Eating Disorders during the past 8 years of work with bulimic adolescents and adults and their spouses and families. I also describe typical impasses as they arise in family therapy in BN, both impasses arising *between* the therapist and the couple or family and impasses arising *within* the couple or family as therapy continues.

Characteristics of the Bulimic Family

Minuchin et al. (1978) found four patterns in psychosomatic families presenting with anorexia nervosa, diabetes mellitus, and asthma. These were initially described as enmeshment, overprotectiveness, rigidity, and poor conflict resolution. *Enmeshment* referred to overly rich emotional connections between family members, usually parent and symptomatic offspring, and poor boundaries between generational subsystems of the family. *Overprotectiveness* referred to the abundance of caretaking and monitoring behaviors in the clinical families in their research project; individual autonomy was low and family members rapidly suppressed differences. *Rigidity* was their term for the strong loyalty to (or intolerance of) changes in long-term family rules and behavior patterns (even after these patterns had long ceased to be functional). *Poor conflict resolution* described these families' tendency to avoid, suppress, or detour significant differences, with chronic low-level tension resulting from unresolved disagreement. These four structural or organizational characteristics were subsequently found in families presenting with the problem of BN (Roberto 1986; Root et al. 1986).

To these organizational characteristics, four other characteristics were subsequently added: *disqualification* of challenges that are foreign to the family's long-term values (Selvini-Palazzoli 1978); *three-way matrimony* (a form of triangulation) between symptomatic family members and their parents (Roberto 1986; Selvini-Palazzoli 1978); strong *self-sacrifice* (Roberto 1987); appearance-consciousness and a *drive for success* (Roberto 1987, 1988; Schwartz et al. 1985). These eight characteristics tend to interfere with important coping mechanisms such as spontaneity, creative problem solving, flexibility, and openness to alternative solutions.

Paradox of the Therapist's Role

When a family with a bulimic member requests treatment for self-induced purging, an immediate dilemma is created by their entry into the therapeutic context. On the one hand, the treatment team represents potential for help and change (cessation of purging). On the other hand, the new metasystem of family plus therapists imposes a challenge to the family's frequently chronic and invariant methods of coping with problems. Tremendous stress can be produced by this early "mismatch" between the agents of change (the treatment team) and an essentially rigid family system. The stress is intensified when the bulimic individual's symptoms are severe, because active intervention is often necessary to curtail purging and may entail extreme measures such as hospitalization, at-home directives, or increased frequency of therapy sessions.

I have identified three common impasses (or reflexive loops) that emerge between treatment team and family as a function of this mismatch. These impasses are interactional moves by one or more family members in therapy that serve to prevent the bulimic patient from disrupting the rigid, enmeshed, overprotective marital or family organization. The interactional moves create reflexive and recurring "loopings" of behavior between therapist and family, without yielding clear solutions.

Impasses in the Therapist-Family Metasystem

"Don't Wash Your Dirty Linen in Public"

Therapists entering into early-stage treatment with the family of a bulimic patient tend to overlook the strong mutual protectiveness the family members maintain toward one another. The overly permeable internal boundaries between parents and children, husbands and wives, and grandparents and parents require a relatively thick *external* boundary or "rubber fence" around the family (Wynne et al. 1958). Consultants are viewed as outsiders, even for families who appear polite and compliant. Efforts to maintain the boundary with "outsiders" can lead to secretiveness and fear of self-disclosure. For example, a father may hide the fact that his own father was emotionally abusive, fearing that this fact will "make the family look bad."

A therapist who accepts this "don't wash your dirty linen in public" stance may begin to replicate this behavior by avoiding interventions that could cause the family to feel exposed. For example, he or she may refrain from hospitalizing a severe purger out of concern that the rest of the family would be embarrassed. Therapist protectiveness helps reinforce the thick boundaries with the outside world, which can in turn support family secretiveness. This reflexive loop may persist well into treatment and produce therapeutic failure or impasse. Therapists must "push against" fear of exposure by acknowledging that beneath the polite exterior there is much to tell. Further, the therapist can accrue leverage with family overprotectiveness by explaining that to teach the bulimic patient how to be direct and take initiative, parents will have to be direct and take initiatives (however embarrassed they are).

"No Big Deal"

Self-sacrifice, a willingness to give up individual needs and goals for the perceived good of the group, is a strong value in families of individuals with eating disorders (Selvini-Palazzoli 1978) and, indeed, in many enmeshed families. This value creates a tendency to focus on one another with frequent nurturant (at times interspersed with controlling) responses between family members. In the another-focus context, many individuals become oblivious to their own distress. Over time, bulimic patients and other family members become accustomed to minimizing emotional upset, and there can be an intellectualized, removed quality to personal discussions. For example, a young woman can calmly describe having her colon resectioned after years of infection following laxative abuse.

Therapists often fail to respond to profound minimization of affect and "no big deal" behavior. Instead, they repeatedly give advice or participate in insight-oriented discussions that do not influence binge-eating or purging behavior. At this impasse, a therapist must "get underneath" ingrained self-sacrificial attitudes and help to highlight individual emotional distress so that it can be addressed. At times, the therapist may need to use his or her own emotional response—his or her own self—to help a bulimic patient and her family access their own distress. For example, showing his or her own concern, shock, or fear of death may help reactivate the family's suppressed anxiety.

"You Promised Us a Rose Garden"

When improvement of bulimic symptoms occurs, spouses and family members often appear disappointed. They may perceive small but realistic increments in self-control and mood as insufficient or transitory. This response reflects the drive for achievement, success, and perfection characteristic of families with patients with eating disorders. For example, the parents of a teenager who has a chronic history of laxative abuse and colitis may fail to notice when she is symptom-free for a month. There may even be complaints that "things are basically still the same" or that therapy has gone on too long for such minor shifts. This success/ perfection impasse is common in late-stage treatment because the patient's self-care and self-esteem have improved but are judged "not good enough."

> Elaine, a 34-year-old obese woman, required care for severe binge eating and vomiting. Her husband complained of his own deeply depressed mood and hyperirritability. The couple attended marital sessions for 4 months, during which many systemic changes occurred. Elaine binged less, lost 10 pounds, vomited once per week or less frequently, and was more interested in her husband; her husband sought her out for companionship; and both were less harsh and demanding with their 10-year-old son. The therapist began pointing out to them these significant therapeutic gains. Both Elaine and her husband expressed disappointment and deep pessimism about the future and renewed their explosive bickering.

It is a painful experience for a success-driven individual and family when improvement occurs and does not resemble the magical "rose garden" for which they wished. To the contrary, behavioral and attitudinal change require hard work and attention. Families of patients with BN must learn to acknowledge negative emotions, risk direct requests, take action to reactivate stagnant relationships, correct mistaken assumptions, take differing positions, and separate. Herein lies the rub. To a patient and spouse or family, although the severe symptoms of bulimia were frightening, they seemed simply to appear and did not require deliberate effort. In contrast, regaining self-control and making change is tiring and burdensome. As one husband put it at termination of treatment, "I thought there was gold at the end of the rainbow . . . now I find it's kind of scattered all around me somewhere."

This impasse is a sad one and tugs at our fantasies of a perfect world, the happy family, and supermen and superwomen. The simplest therapeutic solution amplifies the family's distress, with the therapist agreeing that it is a difficult world, marriage is complicated, personal change is demanding, and family life is emotionally stressful. The therapist augments the fatalism instead of directly challenging the underlying perfectionism and thereby makes a space for the family to become more realistic.

Impasses in Marital and Family Therapy of Bulimia

The reflexive looping of mutual enabling behavior that occurs between clinical family and consultant also takes place within families and couples with a patient with an eating disorder (J.A. Harkaway, 1987, unpublished observations). Within marriages and families, these loops of interaction are frequently focused on the bulimic individual's figure, the status of her health, eating and purging behavior, or her efforts to assert herself and obtain support. Overprotective and controlling interactions, enmeshment, lack of conflict resolution, self-sacrifice, and emphasis on performance and success can easily draw the bulimic patient into relational struggles that distract her from the importance of self-management. On the other hand, she focuses on certain relational struggles instead of clarifying and expressing her individual needs.

There are four marital and family impasses that arise when a bulimic spouse begins to exert self-control and to express her opinions directly rather than secretly gorging or purging.

"What Goes Up Must Come Down"

The overly rich emotional connectedness between a bulimic individual and her partners creates an interdependency like the meshing of gears. When one member shifts position, it is inevitable that another shifts positions as well. This movement in tandem is most directly observed in dyads, such as husband and wife or daughter and father. If the shift made by the bulimic patient is toward greater self-expression, self-control, and autonomy, the "connected" parties inevitably experience a shift as well and become less controlled and more distressed. For example, as a depressed wife becomes more self-confident, her husband may appear clinically depressed. From a Bowenian viewpoint, partners are so poorly differentiated that there is no existential "space" for one to change without the other experiencing disruption.

> Joan began purging at age 35 after she received gastric stapling in an effort to control chronic compulsive overeating since age 16. She induced vomiting daily, and her weight decreased from 200 pounds to 145 pounds. In marital psychotherapy, she began to control her vomiting and describe long-term problems of intimidation and neglect by her husband and family. As she grew more self-appreciative and effective, her husband, Ross (also age 35 and obese), began to eat uncontrollably,

gained 30 pounds, and suffered nightmares and repeated episodes of crying, but he "didn't know why."

This impasse in marital or family treatment calls for substantial challenges by the consultant to create an affective "space" between the bulimic patient and her spouse, parent, grandparent, or child. The challenges must be made with an acceptance of the family's connectedness so that the mutual focus is positively connoted rather than pathologized. One method for creating interpersonal distance is to ask spouses or family members to "make the sacrifice" of watching abrupt changes in behavior impassively without "giving way to panic or despair." This intervention makes use of familial protectiveness and self-sacrifice to challenge enmeshment, accepting one pattern while disrupting the other.

"Better Dead Than Red"

Rigidity or intolerance of differences becomes visible in marriages and families when a bulimic patient shows signs of change. Growing tension is generated by the triadic stressors of chronic dysfunction, movement toward further individuation, and the pressure of responding to purging and illness. Root et al. (1986) noted that a bulimic family is "a conservative system that readily returns to a former balance" (p. 49). Although past efforts may have failed to provide solutions to problems of overconnection, self-suppression, and excessive emphasis on obligation and performance, these patterns are at least familiar and known. Spouses, parents, and offspring may view individuation as rebellion or as a threat to the existence of the family.

Many of these patients and families have memories of especially painful or traumatic events that are so deeply hidden that they constitute secrets. Clinical observation at the Center for Eating Disorders has shown that, for example, in one 5-year sample of hospitalized bulimic young women, more than 75% reported sexual molestation or physical abuse by family elders or a close friend of the family or husband. Many of these patients' mothers had also been sexually or physically abused (Roberto 1986). Root et al. (1986) reported similar findings.

As a bulimic patient's self-awareness grows, previously hidden memories emerge during psychotherapy, and her secretiveness and self-punitiveness may be deeply disrupted. A daughter whose previous position was as a compliant confidante to her mother may reveal her mother's story of rape. A son whose task was to be self-sufficient and further the achievements of his family may begin to confront his father about allowing the paternal grandfather to intimidate the family. A spouse or parent intent on trying to stay the same can become hostile and resentful when rules or secrets are suddenly exposed and challenged. He or she will then convey to the bulimic individual that it is better to have the symptoms than to betray long-term family rules. The implicit message is "better dead than red."

> Heloise entered marital therapy at the age of 37 for daily laxative abuse, food restriction leading to chronic low weight, and suicidal tendencies. She was reluctant to inform her father and stepmother (her mother was deceased), who resided far away, of her hospitalization and chronic panic-level anxiety. In early marital sessions, she revealed painful memories of her father's drug addiction, her mother's insistence on compliance, and a sister's uncontrollable compulsive rituals. She also reported that her husband felt forced to leave home at age 16 because of explosive-rage problems with his father.
>
> Her husband quickly grew cold and contemptuous, forbade her to "complain" further about his family, and pointed out that the harsh conditions in his home had provided the motivation and aggression necessary for him to become a successful financier. Her sister, when notified of her crisis, informed Heloise that she was too busy to fly in for a family meeting and informed her that she had always been a disturbed and vindictive child.

Impasses of rigidity in a marriage or family with a bulimic individual require intervention focusing on familial loyalties and fear of change. The consultant should realize that this fear, although suppressed, involves an expectation of family *dissolution*—further loss and chaos—should differences be accepted and supported. Therefore, spouses and families respond to understanding and acceptance of their dedication and efforts to "hold on." They can be told that they have good reason to discourage unpleasant disclosures and that they will have to proceed very slowly with frequent checks to assess their ability to tolerate the stress. Consultants who confront a family about its rigid responses of "too much too soon" will be extruded, much like the differentiating symptom bearer.

"She's a Sick Woman"

Researchers have noted the presence of detouring individual differences that lead to conflict in families of persons with eating disorders. Simple avoidance is apparent in families of patients with anorexia nervosa, but families of patients with BN develop more complex methods to try to control their intermittently high levels of stress. Repeated efforts to suppress or maneuver around differences prevent opinions from becoming acknowledged disagreements. Such maneuvers can appear hostile and forbidding or benevolent and reassuring.

Frequently, a focus on the patient's bulimic symptoms is used to skirt relational differences. As a result, explicit conflict is suppressed and solutions cannot be found for chronic disagreements. This characteristic process is called *poor conflict resolution.*

Premature closure is behavior that abruptly ends an emerging dispute without sustaining it long enough for negotiation. Closure is produced impulsively, through explosions of anger, physically leaving a scene, withdrawal into passivity or depression, ritualistic lecturing, or a decision to eat on a binge and purge (Roberto 1987).

These two problems of conflict produce an impasse such as that typified by the comment "she's a sick woman," which serves to suppress constructive conflict and problem solving.

> Gwen, a 35-year-old obese working mother, requested help for her severely conflictual marriage to Pete. After beginning marital therapy, she confided that she had been binge eating and vomiting since age 16 and had never disclosed this. As a structure was planned to lower her calories, normalize her mealtimes, and provide alternatives to vomiting, marital arguments worsened.
>
> Gwen found herself increasingly preoccupied with frightening memories of severe beatings by her parents and sexualized ridicule by her mother. Afraid to inform her parents of the memories, she began to relate them to her husband, only to finally explode in rage. Afterward, the intensity of her outbursts frightened them both further. In the fourth month of marital therapy, during a marital fight, Pete announced suddenly that Gwen "had something wrong with her." Gwen agreed that her anger probably meant she was sick.

Impasses based on poor conflict resolution or premature closure signal that a bulimic patient and her spouse or family are attempting to control the level of emerging disagreement. The resulting lack of negotiation or new solutions, however, adds to the tension and intensifies fear that discussing differences will only make the situation worse. If the therapist accepts conflict detouring or premature closure, the marital partners or family may begin to experience hopelessness, believing that their understanding of one another will never improve. This impasse frequently causes the patient to drop out of therapy, with the patient (or a delegated family member) announcing that therapy has only caused more pain, "made things worse," or dredged up past issues that have nothing to do with the bulimia "now."

Therefore, consultants should take a firm stand on the side of sustaining disagreements. The therapist normalizes conflict as an unfortunately universal part of marital and family intimacy and frames it as a crucial forerunner of making more healthy family decisions. The intense emotionality that may appear is also normalized, even if it is disorganized or inappropriately expressed, and the patient and family are told that emotionality feels frightening only because they "are not used to it yet." Bulimic patients respond to this strategy experientially. Many purgers who are temporarily purge-free report waves of affect that seem overwhelming during the periods when he or she used to vomit, abuse laxatives, or exercise.

"The Big Chill"

The impasse known as "the big chill" occurs when a symptom bearer or others allied with him or her directly offers information that is new, highly sensitive, or otherwise disturbing. Such interactions are likely to occur in middle-stage therapy, when the bulimic patient has become confident enough to take a firm position and be more assertive. Family members or spouses frequently move to disqualify the assertive position to lessen its impact. Typical disqualifications can be bland, as when participants attempt to change the subject, or hostile, as when they offer criticisms or threats. The effect of this impasse is to forcibly push a newly assertive patient into a sense of guilt or worthlessness and away from increased initiative.

> Belinda (age 45) sought therapy for herself with a 12-year history of self-induced vomiting, a gastric ulcer, and uncontrollable vaginismus. As she and her husband, Fred, explored the course of her bulimia, she became rapidly aware of chronic relational stress in her family of origin. She recalled emotional maltreatment by her older brother and harsh strictness in her father. Although Fred avoided offering questions or comments, 6 months into marital therapy she reported an uneasy feeling that physical abuse had occurred in her childhood. As her parents were deceased, two sessions were held with a brother and two

younger married sisters, in a search for any clues. All siblings pronounced the discussions mystifying, avoided Belinda between sessions, and radiated a palpable aura of antagonism. Shortly afterward, she remembered that her father had administered daily enemas to her and her two sisters from infancy until each reached the age of 13. The chilling behavior of her siblings caused Belinda to question for some time whether the enemas had "really happened" despite the fact that one sister still possessed the equipment.

Impasses of disqualification are powerful obstacles to treatment because the attachments between a symptomatic individual and spouse or family are deeper and broader than those between patient and therapist. Faced with a forcible recoil, most bulimic patients choose to accommodate themselves to the disqualifying marriage or family and subsequently relapse. The supportive therapist and antagonistic family appear on opposite "sides" during such periods.

Therefore, it is advisable that a systemic message acknowledging the "split" be sent to the couple or family. The therapist points out their wish to suppress disturbing ideas and to prevent trouble. At the same time, the symptom bearer is reminded that he or she may return to self-punitive behavior and ill health if he or she continues to accommodate his or her behavior to the family or spouse. Such messages are framed as a therapeutic dilemma for the patient and his or her partners, and no immediate recommendations are offered. The anxiety generated by the message, coupled with the patient's earlier gains in self-confidence, is usually powerful enough to combat disqualification.

Plans as Therapeutic Impasse

Bulimia nervosa and anorexia nervosa have historically shown a high rate of relapse. Variable-length follow-up studies of treated anorexic patients have shown only 17–40% of them to be symptom-free within the first year (Garfinkel and Garner 1982). Thirty-four percent require more than one hospitalization in the process (Rollins and Piazza 1981). Frequency of relapse for patients with BN is less clear. The most recent family-outcome study (Schwartz et al. 1985) found that at follow-up after a mean of 16 months, 9 of 29 (31%) closed cases were symptomatic (purging once per week or more). Thus, relapse is common even in the most innovative treatment programs. I believe that relapse is a behavior—not an outcome—in bulimia.

Root et al. (1986) distinguished *relapse* from *collapse*, with relapse referring to deliberate binging and purging as a form of deliberately reverting to old coping mechanisms and collapse referring to binging and purging without awareness as a form of deterioration. From the family-systems viewpoint, relapse is a relational behavior that propels spouses and families into returning to their previous rigid patterns of organization. Schwartz et al. (1985, p. 302) stated that the social isolation, dependency, and self-denial of bulimic patients will be reactivated frequently during late-stage therapy. On one level, a return to binge eating and purging after becoming symptom-free represents reinstatement of the characteristic behaviors and attitudes that are part of bulimia. This reinstatement can be either deliberately planned or brought about through despair and loss of competence.

Nineteen-year-old Maeve, a high school senior, was referred to an eating-disorders inpatient unit with normal-weight bulimia. She binged and purged equally often, 3–4 times per day, abused alcohol to the point of blackouts at least biweekly, abused diet pills, and was sexually promiscuous. Individual and extended family meetings were held during her one-month hospital stay and for 11 months after. Guarded and secretive, her adoptive parents and siblings stated that they pitied Maeve for her illness and for the embarrassing events that caused her biological parents (friends of her adoptive parents) to give her up.

During the 11 months of follow-up study, Maeve made many gains, including a decision to discuss her adoption with her biological parents, improved autonomy from her protective parents, initiation of personal discussion with her siblings, and cessation of purging and alcohol and pill use. At the end of the spring, Maeve realized that the coming autumn would see the end of financial assistance from her parents. Her career plans required that she attend college away from her hometown. In the face of the coming psychological separation, Maeve became highly depressed and resumed binging, purging, and drinking weekly. Her siblings invited her to drinking parties, and both sets of parents refrained from discussing her graduation and career.

This description of a deliberate return to active purging illustrates that in the process of growing autonomy and individuation, bulimic patients and their significant others may be tempted to "slow down" or forestall further stress by relapsing to old patterns.

On another level, a return to binge eating and purging can be viewed as an escalation of hidden marital and family conflicts by "going one down" and conspicuously losing control. When the patient creates this obstacle to change—often with no apparent provocation as with other impasses—it is similar to a psychotic communication: "Only if you were not what you are can I be what I am not but what I should have been. To help me, you don't have to do anything, it wouldn't help anyway. In order to really help me, you should really *be* what you should have been" (Selvini-Palazzoli et al. 1978, p. 36). By appearing out of control, medically unstable, and disorganized, she sends a message that her partner or family is also ineffective and out of control. Such a message is a powerful weapon for expressing dissatisfaction, and many patients report that it is difficult to give up this "one-down" maneuver because spouses and families pay attention to relapses. In families that are disengaged and even hostile, the temptation to become symptomatic again or even quite ill can be overwhelming at times.

Finally, relapse behavior in middle-stage or late-stage therapy may represent a message directed to the therapist or treatment team. I have identified two treatment conditions under which a return to binge eating and purging is common. The first condition involves an impasse created by the therapist or treatment team advocating or mandating changes. Statements that the patient must stop purging, is being irresponsible, or should work harder to achieve self-control all appear to mandate change. Since a bulimic patient may be the product of an extended family system that is itself quite rigid and performance oriented, she may be quite sensitive on hearing this implied by the therapist. One way to push back against implied expectations is to lose control and appear helpless. The second condition occurs when a therapist becomes overenthused about a slight improvement. Expressions of pleasure or satisfaction when a patient forgoes binging and purging are interpreted as more evidence that the therapist wants something from the patient. Further, she may feel that the treatment team does not understand the tremendous effort involved in cessation of purging or her anxiety about being more direct and, therefore, vulnerable in intimate relationships. For this reason, systemic treatment teams have advocated maintaining guarded enthusiasm when a bulimic patient achieves self-control—tracking the improvement and positively connoting the patient's efforts, but also questioning whether she is strong enough to maintain gains under intense relational pressure (Roberto 1986; White 1983).

Family Impasses After Recovery

Overconnectedness (enmeshment), overprotectiveness, and three-way matrimony (triangulation) yield an extended family that is tightly bonded for at least three generations (Roberto 1986, 1988; Root et al. 1986). As mentioned before, the attachments may appear benevolent or hostile and mutually controlling. Further, an appearance of conflict or disengagement does not mean that the family of a bulimic patient is not overconnected. Hoffman (1981) pointed out that during long periods of time, it is possible for a fused couple or family to reach a state of emotional upheaval leading to temporary disengagement. Nevertheless, organizations of families with bulimic patients are emotionally binding and inappropriately interdependent.

One result of the vertical attachment across generations is triangulation of offspring into the affairs of parents and grandparents—the three-way matrimony. This triangulation is initially expressed by a bulimic patient overfocusing on the needs and wishes of her family, spouse, or in-laws. Other evidence is found in her reluctance to express negative feelings or to challenge intimates in an unpleasant way. Her nonsymptomatic siblings also play their part in the enmeshed family—as the "successful" child, the parents' advocate, the family confidante, or the independent one who never becomes overwhelmed by stress (Roberto 1988).

As a bulimic patient becomes more autonomous and effective, she leaves a gap between herself and her partners. One frequent outcome is the emergence of a new "patient" to take her place and a return to the old family structure. The new symptom bearer may be a sibling who develops an eating disorder or who is suddenly discovered to be suffering from a previously neglected eating disorder. Children of a bulimic mother or father may begin to behave inappropriately, bringing the focus of the extended family onto themselves. One part of a recovering bulimic patient often begins to express unhappiness, marital dissatisfaction, depression, or substance-abuse problems. These characteristics all reflect the tendency of families with bulimic patients to triangulate family members into inadequately developed marriages and previous individuation failures.

Lena was a 42-year-old married woman who practiced a trade at which she was self-employed and managed a household with two children and a husband in the Army. Despite her intelligence, talent, and competence, she believed herself to be an uninteresting and inadequate woman. Her first husband, who died in a vehicle accident, had been sexually promiscuous. Her second husband, a veteran of the war in Vietnam, suffered from posttraumatic stress syndrome and was emotionally abusive.

Lena had been raised in a traditional Midwestern family in which her brother was given most parental consideration, whereas she and her two sisters were neglected and criticized if they ate too much. She had restricted her food since she was 16 years old, and she purged daily with laxatives.

In marital psychotherapy, Lena found self-esteem and began listening to her own observations and responses to her marriage and family, rather than those of her husband and father. She informed her parents that she would speak to them more as an adult and wished for their respect. She also challenged her husband to control his anger and address his disorder, refusing to support any more abuse.

In the 6 months that followed, Lena remained in recovery at a clinically normal weight and without purging. The couple seemed to tolerate her increased self-worth and assertiveness without crisis. Nevertheless, Lena's 11-year-old son appeared sadder about the atmosphere at home, stopped eating, and lost so much weight that he approached clinical anorexia.

It is necessary to prepare spouses and families of origin for this eventuality. Spouses are told that having an assertive, healthy wife or husband may be unsettling and may even highlight previously hidden self-doubts and insecurities in other family members. Parents and extended families are told that they will begin to notice marital issues or unresolved familial dilemmas, perhaps for the first time. It is advisable to predict these responses to recovery, but some families also require an addendum to treatment that addresses the stalemated parental marriages and cross-generational binds. Schwartz et al. (1985) pointed out that this additional treatment does not necessarily require a search for increased intimacy between parents. I agree, but the parents may be forced to address the nature of their marriage explicitly and make renewed decisions. Further, specific cross-generational problems may need to be explicitly discussed —for example, whether the parental couple will take an aging grandparent into their home or offer financial aid to an adult sibling who is between jobs.

Typically, the cross-generational addendum constitutes brief problem-focused family therapy for its own purpose. Intervention is not as widespread as earlier phases focused on the bulimic patient. If a new symptom bearer emerges who is not a sibling of the recovering bulimic, generations should be kept more separate by holding marital sessions or parent-grandparent sessions. When symptoms are severe, as with a divorced parent who becomes depressed and suicidal, individual psychotherapy is desirable.

Summary

The unique organization of families with a bulimic member includes numerous specific behaviors and beliefs about intimacy, cohesiveness, the value of conflict, the importance of success, and the nature of change. A systemic and cross-generational understanding of these families identified eight different emotional processes that accompany severe binge eating and purging. In the context of therapy, the interface between couple and consultant or family and consultant is expected to produce unavoidable impasses.

Between a therapist or treatment team and a clinical family, there are three impasses that cause special difficulty: reluctance to reveal information in public, minimization and denial of severe distress in therapy, and dismissal of real improvement as not good enough. Between spouses or between patients and family, four common impasses include deterioration in significant others when a bulimic patient improves, intolerance of challenges, attributions of sickness, and disqualification. These impasses call for highly specific responses from the therapist and treatment team to prevent repeated looping of maladaptive behavior.

Relapse itself can be considered a treatment impasse. Renewed binge eating or purging has implications for how a bulimic patient sees herself, her marriage and family, and her therapy. Therapists have a clear role to play in responding to covert messages, making them explicit, and creating a context that addresses hidden fears.

Finally, negotiating the family life-cycle without an ill daughter or wife is more complicated than families expect. In many circumstances, it is advisable to orient spouses and families toward newly autonomous relationships and draw out the implications for the individual growth that must now occur.

In general, rather than avoiding impasses, it is more effective to predict them and plan specific strategies to manage them. The family consultant's position can directly influence their outcome—deterioration or transformation.

References

Garfinkel PE, Garner DM: Anorexia Nervosa: A Multidimensional Perspective. New York, Brunner/Mazel, 1982

Hoffman L: Foundations of Family Therapy. New York, Basic Books, 1981

Minuchin S, Rosman B, Baker L: Psychosomatic Families: Anorexia Nervosa in Context. Cambridge, MA, Harvard University Press, 1978

Roberto LG: Bulimia: the transgenerational view. Journal of Marital and Family Therapy 12:231–240, 1986

Roberto LG: Bulimia: transgenerational family therapy, in Eating Disorders and Family Therapy. Edited by Harkaway JA. New York, Aspen, 1987, pp 1–11

Roberto LG: The vortex: siblings in the eating disordered family, in Siblings in Therapy. Edited by Lewis KG, Kahn MD. New York, WW Norton, 1988, pp 297–313

Rollins N, Piazza E: Anorexia nervosa: a quantitative approach to follow-up. J Am Acad Child Psychiatry 20: 167–183, 1981

Root M, Fallon P, Friedrich W: Bulimia: A Systems Approach to Treatment. New York, WW Norton, 1986

Russell G: Bulimia nervosa: an ominous variant of anorexia nervosa. Psychol Med 9:429–448, 1979

Schwartz R, Barrett MJ, Saba G: Family therapy of bulimia, in Handbook of Psychotherapy for Anorexia and Bulimia. Edited by Garner DM, Garfinkel PE. New York, Guilford, 1985, pp 280–310

Selvini-Palazzoli M: Self-starvation: From Individual to Family Therapy in the Treatment of Anorexia Nervosa. New York, Jason Aronson, 1978

Selvini-Palazzoli M, Boscolo L, Cecchin G, et al: Paradox and Counterparadox: A New Model in Therapy of the Family in Schizophrenic Transaction. New York, Jason Aronson, 1978

White M: Anorexia nervosa: a transgenerational system perspective. Fam Process 22:255–273, 1983

Wynne LC, Ryckoff IM, Day J, et al: Pseudomutuality in the family relations of schizophrenics. Psychiatry 21:205–220, 1958

Chapter 5

Family Treatment in the Day Hospital

**D. BLAKE WOODSIDE, M.D., M.Sc.,
F.R.C.P.(C)
LORIE SHEKTER-WOLFSON, M.S.W., C.S.W.**

Chapter 5

Family Treatment in the Day Hospital

In Chapters 5 and 6, we discuss aspects of working with families in the setting of an intensive day-hospital program (DHP) for treating eating disorders. The DHP is located on the grounds of a large urban teaching center, but it is geographically separate from other psychiatric facilities. Patients are admitted to the DHP for a minimum of 8 and a maximum of 16 weeks. The program runs from 11:00 A.M. until 6:30 P.M. The DHP is a group treatment program, with no individual therapy. In fact, patients are required to discontinue contact with individual therapists while they attend the DHP. The main focus of the program is nutritional rehabilitation. Most of the groups focus on the issues of normal eating, weight, and shape. Patients eat two meals and one snack in the day hospital, and they are responsible for their own breakfast and for their meals on weekends.

Issues that are not directly food-related are addressed, but with less intensity than nutritional issues. There are groups on assertion, leisure and time management, relationships, and sexuality; however, these are a more peripheral part of the program, primarily because of the program's short duration.

The inclusion of family therapy in the DHP was initially a controversial issue. Not only was the program designed to consist primarily of group therapy, but all of the patients were intended to be adults—18 years of age or older. It was expected that most of the patients would be living away from home at the time of admission and, therefore, might not be in a position to benefit from such therapy (Bruch 1979; Root et al. 1986). An initial decision was made to limit family contact to an assessment only (to understand the patient in her family environment) and give the family an opportunity to meet the therapeutic team and learn about the program.

Experience soon proved, however, that the issue of family therapy would have to be reexamined. Many of our patients still live at home. The rest are either living on their own, married, or living in common-law arrangements. The latter patients are still emotionally connected to their family of origin, often in pathological ways.

As a result, the role of the family became more prominent in the overall treatment of the patient. It was decided that the family would be seen for the preassessment interview, where the entire treatment team would be present, followed by a longer assessment performed by the family therapy team. The family would then be seen regularly if possible during the course of the patient's treatment in the DHP.

In this chapter, we outline, in some detail, the family work that is offered in the DHP, including a review of the preassessment and assessment process, family treatment goals, and termination. Case vignettes are presented to illustrate the process of family treatment in this setting.

The Preassessment

The family preassessment occurs in the setting of the general admission preassessment. The family is invited to the group preassessment for approximately one half hour after the patient has been interviewed individually, usually by the psychiatrist. This is an extremely important part of the preassessment, because the entire treatment team gets an opportunity to observe the identified patient in the context of her family system. It also allows the family to meet the treatment team; further contact usually takes place only with the family therapist.

The patient is asked to invite her family to the preassessment interview. Often, the patient will only include those family members who are still living at home. Other times, the patient may include in-laws or friends.

If the patient is married or living in a common-law arrangement, the spouse is invited. If the patient is homosexual and has an active current partner, the partner will also be invited. We have found that the pattern of who is invited to this initial meeting may be as revealing as the meeting itself.

The preassessment family interview borrows from Haley (1977) some of the stages of a first interview, including the social and problem stages. Given the brief duration of this interview, the social stage is often more brief than would be ideal. It is important, however, to make the family members feel comfortable, because further work with the patient or family will be less effective if the first interchange is disenchanting.

The problem stage asks what family members know about why the patient has come to be assessed. The question will have a different impact on families who have known about the problem for some time than on families who have been told about the problem only recently. Many patients with bulimia nervosa have "secret" bulimia, and families are sometimes informed of the problem on their way to the DHP assessment. In one case, the parents were told that they were seeing a gastroenterology specialist about their daughter's vomiting. When the family arrived at the hospital, she announced on their way to the DHP that she was bulimic. Naturally, the parents had many questions to ask during the preassessment interview about the nature of their daughter's illness.

Examples of the questions asked of families during the preassessment family interview include the following: What is each family member's perception of the patient's problem? When did they first become aware of the problem? What have they each done to help the patient overcome his or her problem?

Following the problem stage, each family member is asked about goals. In addition to the obvious answer, "get rid of the eating disorder," more specific questions are asked regarding the possibility of the patient gaining weight and the likely changes in dietary habits that will occur. For a family that is particularly health-conscious or has specific food avoidances, these issues can be important.

The preassessment ends with a decision by both the team and the patient on the suitability of the patient for admission to the DHP. If the patient is accepted, a family-assessment date is set, and the family is given the Family Assessment Measure (FAM) questionnaires (Skinner et al. 1983) to complete before this assessment.

The Family Assessment

The assessment interview normally takes place just prior to the patient's admission to the DHP. It is usually 90 minutes long. Married patients or patients with significant relationships have separate assessments scheduled for their spouses and their families of origin. The reason for this is threefold. First, information can be obtained from the respective families more readily without the families confusing the issue by comparing different family styles. Although these differences ultimately provide important information, some of this will have been observed during the preassessment interview. If it seems appropriate, we schedule conjoint sessions at later times during the admission.

Second, the respective families are given feedback on their FAM results during the assessment. This information is family-specific and should only be given to the family members involved.

Third, it is important to establish clear boundaries for the two families (Minuchin and Fishman 1981) at the outset of treatment. We have observed that many of our patients have had difficulty in differentiating their current relationship from their relationship with their family of origin. Minuchin et al. (1978) described this as enmeshment. Members of enmeshed subsystems may be handicapped in that the heightened sense of belonging requires a major yielding of autonomy. Often, issues of autonomy are disguised by such "overcaring." By clearly marking boundaries between subsystems, concerns about autonomy will become more apparent.

In addition, the family of origin sometimes wishes to be included in the interviews with the patient's current family. Sargent et al. (1985) commented on the dual nature of this response, which includes a sense of responsibility but also a lack of trust of one another. Often, family members who felt obligated to be present at all meetings are relieved to be informed that this is incorrect.

These considerations make the decision of whom to invite to the assessment a powerful intervention in its own right. This is part of what Stern et al. (1981) described as the "battle for structure" in the early phases of family therapy. During this phase, the family tests the therapist and therapy team to see whether they are strong enough to maintain authority. "Winning" the battle for structure means that the therapist has established the therapeutic situation as his or her domain, in which the therapist decides what is and what is not therapeutic. This must be done without humiliating the family members or rendering them passive.

Assessment Format

The assessment has a semistructured format. This includes a fairly standardized assessment process (Minuchin 1974) that addresses a description of the family structure, the system's flexibility, boundaries, family life-cycle, and the family developmental stage. A questionnaire on family history and eating patterns has been developed to help collect important information about the family, especially pertaining to weight, food, general eating patterns, and the family's involvement in the eating disorder. Areas assessed include various family members' own preoccupation with weight, shape, and exercise; views of others' weights and shapes; and the nature and settings of meals. This type of information has proved invaluable in aiding family therapists to understand an identified patient's preoccupation with weight and food. One patient, a 25-year-old woman, living at home, had a father who was very preoccupied with weight. His involvement with his daughter included a daily workout in the gym with her. He weighed himself daily, the scales being kept just outside his daughter's bedroom door. The introduction of a treatment program for eating disorders interfered with the normal family routine and exposed the existence of a significant secondary reason for the patient to remain preoccupied with weight and shape.

A similar questionnaire has been developed to guide the assessment of couples. This assessment includes an evaluation of a spouse's or boyfriend's eating habits, patterns of exercise, and preoccupation with weight. The views of the spouse are often as problematic as the views of the family of origin. One of our patients felt that she had to leave the program because the gym workouts with her boyfriend were their main social time together, and she had been asked to reduce her exercise as part of her treatment. Although the boyfriend denied that their reduced exercise was a problem, she clearly had a different view of the situation.

We use the FAM-III questionnaire (Skinner et al. 1983) as a research and clinical tool. The FAM-III is a four-point, forced-choice, self-report measure that examines seven dimensions of family functioning—task accomplishment, role performance, communication, affective expression, control, values, and norms. These dimensions were characterized as part of the development of the Process model of family functioning (Steinhauer et al. 1984).

The FAM-III assesses the family from three different perspectives: 1) the general scale, focusing on the level of health pathology in the family from a systems perspective; 2) the dyadic-relationships scale, focusing on relationships between specific pairs of dyads; and 3) the self-rating scale, which focuses on the individual's perception of his or her functioning in the family.

Families normally complete the FAM questionnaire between the preassessment and the formal assessment. At the end of the formal assessment, the FAM profiles are reviewed with the family. We use the FAM to delineate both family strengths and problems and to help the family avoid blaming themselves for the eating disorder. This emphasis on both strengths and weaknesses can assist the therapist on several levels. First, the identification of family strengths can provide leverage to propel the family toward change. Second, the emphasis on strengths can help normalize a family system that has been preoccupied with pathology. Finally, the continued awareness of strengths as well as weaknesses aids the therapist in maintaining the balanced view of families necessary for establishing a therapeutic alliance and minimizing pessimism on the part of the families and therapist (Steinhauer et al. 1984).

Issues Specific to the Family Assessment

The family-assessment process is often difficult for both the patient and the family. It is a confirmation that the illness exists and that intervention is required. In the family of a patient with anorexia nervosa, there has often been an intense struggle over food, usually for several months or years. Typically, it is the parents or caretakers of these patients who have sought help, rather than the patients themselves. This can provoke a serious unspoken conflict within the family, because our program is voluntary and a patient must state openly that she wishes to enter the program. Often the patient will later struggle with the staff about program details in a fashion similar to the struggle she has had with her family.

Because of the intensity of the underlying, often unspoken conflicts, initial family assessments can be rather formal and superficial. It is not unusual for the family to state that "everything in the family was fine until she became sick."

Families of patients with bulimia nervosa will have a different response, depending on whether the bulimia was acknowledged or secret. A bulimic patient is often uninterested in treatment, particularly if she also suffers from anorexia nervosa or is firmly committed to a dieting lifestyle. The family of a bulimic patient may openly support abnormal eating behaviors such as excessive dieting while harshly condemning the binge eating or purging behaviors that the dieting has produced. Because the conflict about these issues is more open and direct, the parents of bulimic patients often feel less intimidated by the symptom (Haley 1977), and the bulimic patient is sometimes anxious to involve her parents in family therapy.

The secret bulimic patient is more likely to be self-referred. Often such a patient will attempt to avoid family involvement, either because "they don't know anyway" or because "they have nothing to do with the problem." Such patients may tell no one about the preassessment interview or tell only a select few people. We encourage our patients to be open with the family about the problem, and we request that all family members who are available attend at least one family session. Most of our patients eventually agree to this.

The focus of the assessment for the family of the secret bulimic patient is different from that for other families. There is usually a significant amount of time spent on the nature of the illness and the purpose of the program. Information about the illness is often totally new to such a family, who may not have been aware of the nature of the problem until minutes before the assessment. For patients living at home, the family has often noticed unusual occurrences, such as missing food. For patients living on their own, the secrecy issue becomes more important, especially if the patient is at a normal weight and is not obviously ill.

Homework

At the conclusion of the assessment, homework is given to the family. This serves two functions. The first function is to reduce their feeling of helplessness by providing a concrete task that can be performed and be viewed as helpful. The second function is to assess the family's ability to change. Homework connected to the patient's eating behavior is common. Most families find themselves caught up in a rigid, repetitive sequence of interaction with the patient. If there has been open conflict, food has usually been a "safe" way of retaining some connection between family members. For the families of secret bulimic patients, the family sometimes wishes to become suddenly overinvolved, thus making up for lost time.

In a situation where a family has been focusing on "safe" food-related issues to avoid other conflicts, making this arena of conflict unavailable may be a potent but difficult intervention (Schwartz et al. 1985). The process is referred to as *symptom separation* and involves such tasks as not asking about the patient's weight and eating habits or not buying special food for the patient. We target specific problem areas for each patient with the assessment interview. For a family that has been involved in open conflict about the symptoms, we usually describe the task as a "vacation" from the illness.

Many families are relieved to have someone else take charge of the "sick" family member. The degree to which the family is able to appropriately disengage may well be a prognostic factor for the eventual outcome of treatment.

Role of the Family Therapy Team

We usually perform our initial assessment in a family team format, using a one-way mirror. Our team process has been adapted from the Milan model of a five-part session (Tomm 1984). This includes 1) a presession, where the family is reviewed and some preliminary hypotheses are made, based on information available from the preassessment; 2) the interview, where the therapist interviews the family for 45–60 minutes, using our semistructured format; 3) the intersession, where the therapist removes himself or herself from the family to discuss the hypotheses with the team behind the mirror and a message is developed; 4) family feedback, which often takes the form of a statement from the team about either the family process or the FAM feedback and includes homework suggestions; and 5) the postsession, where the therapist and the team discuss the family interview further and decisions are made about the frequency of sessions and the goals for treatment.

This framework has proved invaluable for working with this patient population for several reasons. First, our clinical population is from a significantly disturbed group, not suitable for routine outpatient care, whose only treatment alternative would normally be hospitalization. A break midway through an interview and some objective feedback can significantly reduce therapist "stuckness" and help plan strategies. Second, the team approach emphasizes the group nature of our treatment program and highlights that there will be no secrets between team members and that all information will be shared. Finally, we use the mirror as a teaching tool, as we regularly have students from various disciplines spending time at the DHP. The mirror offers an opportunity for students to observe and work with families in a structured, supervised setting.

Treatment

We make decisions about the nature of a patient's family treatment at the DHP on the basis of several factors. The first is the practical issue of distance. Our program serves a geographically large area, the province of

Ontario, Canada, and we have frequent referrals from outside the province and from the United States. We have had several patients whose families lived in Europe. For such families, the family therapy component of treatment is usually small or nonexistent. For families who are able to attend, the issues addressed depend in large part on who would be able to attend. If siblings are the only family members available, the issues addressed will be different from those addressed when parents are available.

The second factor is the attitude of the patient toward family involvement. Family involvement, although the norm, is not strictly an absolute requisite for admission to the day hospital. With those patients for whom family involvement is viewed with hostility or ambivalence, the approach is to state the program's opinion about the value of family involvement and then continue to encourage family involvement. The issue of families in general is also addressed in the family relationship group (see Chapter 6), and this group is a powerful tool for reducing resistance to family involvement. Most patients will eventually consent to involving their families. Our experience has been that patients who are unable to even tell their immediate family about the illness tend to do rather poorly on the whole. In this regard, even a single session seems to improve the prognosis, probably for reasons external to the content of such a single session.

A third factor that may come into play is the family circumstances of the patient, including the family's previous treatment experiences. For families that have been involved in intensive family treatment, a reduced number of sessions may be recommended to give the family a "therapeutic holiday." Families who are newer to the disorder or its treatment may require more sessions. For patients who are married, concurrent family and marital sessions may take place.

Finally, if a family seems supportive and understanding, it may not be necessary to see the family frequently. Nevertheless, because of the intensive nature of our program, which is suitable for more ill individuals, we have found that most of our families are quite needy and stressed.

More specific goals are described in the next section. We agree with other authors (e.g., Garfinkel and Garner 1982; Vandereycken 1985) who recommend a multidimensional approach to the treatment of eating disorders. Our family therapy occurs in the setting of an intensive group treatment program whose major goal is normalized eating. Our goals for family therapy are formulated with this in mind.

Goals of Family Treatment

In general, the goals of family therapy are first- or second-order change. First-order change occurs when a family adapts to but does not cease its symptomatic functioning. Second-order change occurs when an intervention has disrupted the pattern of symptomatic interaction so that it ceases (Watzlawick et al. 1974). The result of second-order change is that the family no longer requires a symptom to function.

In our program, second-order change is the goal. This is not always realistic. For families who are geographically only able to attend one or no meetings, family change will be limited. Second-order change also seems to be affected by the type of family that we see, that is, whether the family is "perfect," "overprotective," or "chaotic" (Root et al. 1986).

The overprotective family has the slogan "all for one and one for all." Such a family most closely resembles the description of a psychosomatic family by Minuchin et al. (1978). Features of such families include enmeshment, an extreme form of proximity; overprotectiveness, a high degree of concern that all family members have for each other; rigidity, the family's commitment to maintain the status quo; and an inability to resolve conflict. In such a family, the eating disorder allows the patient to stay young and dependent. At the same time, it serves as a way to rebel passively and create "personal space" (Root et al. 1986). Consequently, bulimic behavior need not be a secret in these families. The patient may be overconcerned about one of the parents because of pervasive personal problems, which can include depression or marital distress.

Crisp et al. (1977) noted that in such families, there tends to be an increase in psychoneurotic disturbance in the parents as the affected daughter improves. The superficial appearance of closeness seems to disintegrate as time passes, which is rather similar to what is seen with the perfect family (described later in this section). In such a family, we have concerns for what will happen to other stressed family members once the initial focus on eating is de-emphasized and other issues begin to emerge. Such families may require considerable support at this point in therapy.

Occasionally, a crisis may need to be induced in the overprotective family to aid the process of de-emphasizing food. This can often occur during a meal interview. Our meal interviews are somewhat different from those described by Minuchin (1974), where the goal of the meal session is to transform the issue of the patient suffering from an eating disorder into the drama of a dysfunctional family. Our meal sessions often take place halfway through the patient's stay at the day hospital, rather than as an assessment tool at the beginning of treatment. By the time the patient has spent some time in the day hospital, her eating is usually under better control and weight gain has occurred. The eating issues may be less of a concern. The patient may choose to discuss other problems during or after the meal. This type of process can eventually lead to second-order change if there is sufficient help provided to the stressed individual and the patient feels that there are other support mechanisms available in addition to herself.

An example of this process occurred with a 22-year-old single woman who was living with her widowed mother in a small town. The patient was very worried about her mother, especially since the mother was living on her own while the patient was at the DHP. Although the mother openly encouraged her daughter not to worry, she also gave her just cause to be concerned by complaining of loneliness, chest pains, or poor sleep. This mother worried about her daughter and did little else.

In the session prior to the meal, we attempted to mark some boundaries between the mother and her daughter regarding the appropriateness of their level of worry. Some first-order change was achieved in terms of reducing the mother's degree of worry, but neither the mother nor her daughter seemed able to make any other shifts.

By the time the meal session was set up, the patient's eating was under control. She ate well in front of her mother—a change from before admission. Surprisingly, her mother had considerable difficulty finishing her meal. During the meal, the mother revealed that she had binged and vomited the night before and that this had been a problem for the mother since long before the patient was born. This was a revelation to the patient; she immediately began to focus on the mother, providing her with suggestions as to how to deal with the problem. The mother became unable to focus on her daughter's problem, because it was no longer an issue. The daughter was able to examine how her mother had been unable to acknowledge her own problem and why she, as a daughter, felt obligated to help her. When the therapist gave the mother a homework assignment of getting help for her own problem, the daughter expressed relief and began to differentiate between her own and her mother's problem. With the help of the other patients and hospital staff members, she was gradually able to recognize that her mother's inability to get help for herself was her mother's problem, and this recognition accompanied continued improvements in her eating.

In the "perfect" family, there is intense family loyalty, often to the point of excluding others, including therapists. A perfect family may become perfect patients in therapy, appearing supportive and helpful to the patient but resisting change. According to Root et al. (1986), bulimic symptoms in such a family serve several important functions, including rebellion, being in control, and developing an identity. A young person with no other obvious opportunity to individuate may be resistant to giving up her disorder. The task of the therapist with such a family is to help the family get past the need for perfection and appreciate the need for mistakes and differences. As with the overprotective family, it may be necessary to induce a crisis to bypass the rigidity and conflict avoidance of these families.

Keeping bulimic behavior a secret makes sense to many patients in such families. Merely disclosing the existence of the illness may create a crisis, especially if other family members have been active in maintaining the secret. If the patient can bring herself to disclose her illness to even one other family member, she may have broken an important, implicit family rule, and this can be the start of second-order change. On one occasion, the family of a patient lived a great distance from the DHP, and the disclosure was done on the telephone with the help of the family therapist. In this specific situation, the patient's mother immediately arranged to fly to our center for a meeting.

The chaotic family often resembles substance-abusing families (Stanton and Todd 1982). Rules are inconsistent, one or both parents are unavailable, anger is expressed inappropriately, and there is usually a family history of substance abuse. For the patient from such a family, the eating disorder may provide the patient with the affection and nurturance lacking in the family and become a safe way to express anger (Root et al. 1986).

It is important to provide a different type of assistance for this type of family. Family members will need help to establish more appropriate boundaries; to establish some structure for eating, such as regular meal times; and to obtain extra support from within and outside the family. The chaotic family is often the most difficult to get into the hospital for sessions. Certain members may refuse to attend sessions.

For these families, we have found that first-order change is more attainable than second-order change. Transformation of the family system into a more available, symptom-free system may be an unrealistic goal. We often suggest that patients seek outside friends or groups for support to avoid further disappointment.

At times, although the eating-disordered individual may eventually feel more in control, other family members may feel out of control—for example, if they are drinking excessively. Concerns about conflict and disappointment are usually more on the surface with these families than with other family types.

One 24-year-old patient, living with her boyfriend, came from an alcoholic family. Her parents had divorced, and she had little contact with them prior to admission. Separate conjoint sessions were held with her mother and her father. It was clear that her parents could not meet all of her needs, but some attainable goals were discussed, including setting up meetings between the patient and her parents and organizing holidays and visits with them separately. All concerned felt that the suggestions were helpful, and the patient was instructed to start the process while she was still attending the DHP. The alcohol issue was discussed but not dealt with directly.

In summary, our goals for family treatment are assessed separately for each family. It is important that families be part of the goal-setting process, even though they may have different expectations from the treatment team.

Goals of Couple Treatment

Goals for the treatment of couples are similar in many ways to the goals for families. The intensity of the symptom-maintaining behavior may be greater in a couple than it was in the family of origin. Schwartz et al. (1985) noted that patients with eating disorders tend to marry, cohabit with, or become involved with individuals in primary relationships that allow them to continue their relationship with their eating disorder.

As a result, much time is spent on symptom-separation issues and in gaining an understanding of the role of the symptom in the relationship. In addition, it is not uncommon for the relationship of the patient and her spouse to mirror her relationship with one parent. When the couple makes references to respective parents' relationships, it is important to elucidate not only the similarities but also the differences between the couple's relationship and those of their parents. This will aid them in becoming a truly autonomous subgroup. This will be an ongoing issue if the patient has had difficulty separating from her family of origin.

Patients often feel trapped between the requirements of the program and their responsibilities to their spouse. In one case involving a 24-year-old woman living with her boyfriend of one year, the boyfriend was very involved in the eating problem. His involvement included buying her food, supervising her eating, and hiding her laxatives. In his words, his involvement in her problem was "a way of protecting her from further harm." The boyfriend was unable to hold down a job and was frequently on unemployment insurance. He also was involved sexually outside the relationship. As the patient's eating began to improve in the program, it was suggested that her boyfriend become less involved in her eating. She was initially relieved, but she soon became angry and verbally abusive. At the same time, she began to see some of her friends alone in the evenings, leaving her boyfriend alone at home. Some of her boyfriend's behavior bothered her, but she seemed able to tolerate it. He began to act out increasingly as she improved. Since she was unwilling to leave him, she left the program instead to "save the relationship."

In our experience, boyfriends, spouses, and homosexual lovers can be significant perpetuating factors in the eating disorder. Therefore, we see the involvement of such individuals in the therapeutic and assessment process as extremely important. As the patient changes, the effect will be most keenly felt by those people closest to her. The prognosis is likely to be poor for a patient who refuses to involve such people in her treatment.

Frequency of Sessions

The two main determinants of the frequency of sessions are the treatment goals and the geographic distance that significant others must travel to attend the sessions. For the average 3-month course of DHP treatment, the average number of visits has been six, including the preassessment and the formal assessment. For families living at a distance, the average is probably closer to three visits. For families who live in Toronto (the city of the hospital), more frequent visits are possible.

If the patient is married, it is not unusual for the family of origin to be more involved initially and then less so as the treatment progresses and the couple becomes the focus of treatment.

Sometimes the frequency of sessions is reflective of the patient's progress in the program. Often, extra sessions are scheduled if things are going particularly poorly at home. Such decisions are made together by the treatment team, the family team, and the patient.

Termination

Patients are given an opportunity to set a discharge date for themselves about 1 month prior to their leaving. One final family session is arranged as a wrap-up session. Families are asked to complete another set of FAM questionnaires, and these are presented to the family, comparing the results to the scores obtained on admission.

Scores that show improvement in family function usually provide a significant feeling of accomplishment for the patient and family and may encourage them to continue whatever changes they attempted to make. In families with no change or a worsening of the family's function, some families are distressed whereas others view the situation more realistically. An example of the latter would be an anorexic "perfect" family. Pretesting suggested that most family members viewed family functioning in the strength range on all subscales. Family members were united in their assertion that until the anorexia had developed, they had been a family without problems, and even since it had developed everything had really been fine.

At discharge from the DHP, following six sessions, most scales were moved into the average range. Patients felt that this was an improvement, and each felt more able to talk openly about conflict in the family and her role as an adult daughter. Parents also seemed less threatened by the differences and less determined to portray the family as "perfect."

Some families request ongoing family or couple therapy. Referrals for ongoing family therapy are rarer because of the older age group of the patients. In some cases, requests for marital counseling emanate from the parents of the patient, occasionally some weeks or months after the patient has been discharged. For patients who are married or living in a common-law arrangement, we have a high rate of referral for couple counseling, because these relationships tend to continue to be stressed as the patients continue to change after discharge.

If a final meeting with the family is not possible, an opportunity is set aside to review the posttreatment FAM scores with the patient, and the rest of the family is encouraged to telephone to discuss the results. In the event that a patient leaves the day hospital precipitously, a wrap-up session will be occasionally scheduled after the patient has left to assess the effect of the patient's departure on the family and to provide advice on support or continued therapy that may be desired by the family.

Special Cases

Some patients have tremendous difficulties with boundary issues. For one patient, a 34-year-old woman with a fairly short history of anorexia nervosa plus bulimia nervosa, this was well illustrated by her preassessment interview. She was married, had two children, and lived near her extended family. She was said to have had significant marital problems by her referring physician. She had a close friend who was instrumental in arranging her referral to the DHP.

For her initial assessment, this patient brought her husband, her parents, her brother, his wife, two of her brothers-in-law, an aunt, and the aforementioned friend. She did not bring either of her children, aged 10 and 12. It was decided that, in the interest of clarifying boundaries, it would be appropriate to conduct the preassessment family interview in two parts, interviewing the patient and her husband first and then inviting everyone else.

After this initial meeting, separate sessions were arranged for the patient and her husband, the patient and her family of origin, and the patient and her friend. We also arranged a special meeting for the patient, her husband, and their children.

The purpose of these rather complicated maneuvers was to aid the patient in discerning appropriate boundaries between these various groups. In other cases where the major difficulty seemed to be family disengagement, we would prefer to meet with the family as a whole.

Sibling dyads are frequently informative. Because of the familial nature of the disorders, siblings are not infrequently also affected with the disorder. Sometimes the sibling may have the desired shape of the patient, and there may be intense competition in terms of absolute weight or amount of food consumed. In such cases, intervention is crucial to expose and thus defuse the competition.

This same pattern is occasionally observed in the marriages and common-law relationships of our patients, where there can be frank competition over weight, shape, or diet. Many of the spouses were initially attracted to the patients when the patients were at a much lower weight, sometimes when the patients were emaciated. A significant change in weight or shape can provoke a crisis in the relationship.

Summary

In this chapter, we summarized briefly the type of family intervention provided in the DHP setting. In Chapter 6, we discuss the integration of this treatment with a group focusing specifically on family issues.

References

Bruch H: Eating Disorders: Obesity, Anorexia Nervosa, and the Person Within. New York, Basic Books, 1979

Crisp AH, Harding B, McGuinness B: Anorexia nervosa: psychoneurotic characteristics of parents: relationship to prognosis. J Psychosom Res 118:167–173, 1977

Garfinkel PE, Garner DM: Anorexia Nervosa: A Multidimensional Perspective. New York, Brunner/Mazel, 1982

Haley J: Problem-Solving Therapy. San Francisco, CA, Jossey-Bass, 1977

Minuchin S: Families and Family Therapy. Cambridge, MA, Harvard University Press, 1974

Minuchin S, Fishman HC: Family Therapy Techniques. Cambridge, MA, Harvard University Press, 1981

Minuchin S, Rosman BL, Baker L: Psychosomatic Families: Anorexia Nervosa in Context. Cambridge, MA, Harvard University Press, 1978

Root MPP, Fallon P, Friedrich WN: Bulimia: A Systems Approach to Treatment. New York, WW Norton, 1986

Sargent J, Liebman R, Silver M: Family therapy for anorexia nervosa, in Handbook of Psychotherapy for Anorexia Nervosa and Bulimia. Edited by Garner DM, Garfinkel PE. New York, Guilford, 1985, pp 257–279

Schwartz RC, Barrett ML, Saba G: Family therapy for bulimia, in Handbook of Psychotherapy for Anorexia Nervosa and Bulimia. Edited by Garner DM, Garfinkel PE. New York, Guilford, 1985, pp 280–310

Skinner H, Steinhauer PD, Santa-Barbara J: The family assessment measure. Canadian Journal of Community Mental Health 2:91–105, 1983

Stanton MD, Todd TC (eds): The Family Therapy of Drug Abuse. New York, Guilford, 1982

Steinhauer PD, Santa-Barbara J, Skinner H: The Process model of family functioning. Can J Psychiatry 29:77–88, 1984

Stern S, Whitaker C, Hagemann N, et al: Anorexia nervosa: the hospital's role in family treatment. Fam Process 20:395–408, 1981

Tomm K: One perspective on the Milan systems approach. Journal of Marital and Family Therapy 16:253–271, 1984

Vandereycken W: Inpatient treatment of anorexia nervosa: some research-guided changes. J Psychiatr Res 19:413–422, 1985

Watzlawick P, Weakland J, Fisch R: Change: Principles of Problem Formation and Problem Resolution. New York, WW Norton, 1974

Chapter 6

A Family Relations Group

LORIE SHEKTER-WOLFSON, M.S.W., C.S.W.
D. BLAKE WOODSIDE, M.D., M.Sc.,
F.R.C.P.(C)

Chapter 6

A Family Relations Group

When the day-hospital program (DHP) for treating eating disorders was established, it was felt important that a family-oriented group be included in the treatment program. This decision was partly based on the multidetermined nature of eating disorders (Garfinkel and Garner 1982) and the need to include a family component in treatment. Because a percentage of the patients were expected to be from outside Toronto, the city of the hospital (the DHP is a province-based program), it was felt that traditional family therapy could not be implemented for a significant number of patients. Thus an alternative format had to be considered, and a patient group dealing with family issues—a family relations group—seemed to be the answer.

The original objectives of the family relations group were 1) to help patients understand and begin to deal with family issues that were perpetuating the illness, 2) to help patients recognize that their feelings regarding their families were not crazy or unique, and 3) to encourage patients to challenge others' beliefs about their perceptions of the family's involvement in the disorder.

A fourth objective was added when it became apparent that more traditional family therapy was occurring more regularly than had originally been anticipated. This included helping the patients apply their learning from the group experience both to the family sessions and home situation.

In setting up this group, it became clear that it was somewhat unique. Literature on family groups has usually examined understanding and treating the family as a group (Bell 1961, 1976; Dreikurs 1951) or examined multiple family group therapies (Gritzer and Okun 1983; Strelnick 1977; Wooley and Lewis 1987); however, the intention was to develop a group that helps patients to focus on issues that usually come up in family therapy, including boundary diffusion, indirect communication styles, conflict resolution, and issues specific to the eating disorder, such as the family's involvement in the patient's eating patterns. The term *family relations* was applied to the group to emphasize the interpersonal content.

In this chapter, we examine the composition of the group, its structure, the use of family themes, the implementation of techniques, style of leadership, problems, and therapeutic snares.

Group Composition

The group is composed of all patients involved in the DHP, usually 8–12. As stated before, the average length of admission to the DHP is 3 months, and the patients are admitted and discharged at different times. As a result, the group is open-ended and the composition is always changing.

The family relations group meets on Wednesday afternoons for 1½ hours. Since new members usually begin the program on Monday, they are somewhat integrated into the general group by Wednesday. Patients seem to share little information spontaneously regarding their families. When there are new group members, some time is spent at the beginning of each session introducing the patients' families. Patients are asked to discuss "who is the family," where family members live, and what they do. In addition, they are asked to introduce their current relationships and any other significant persons.

The introductions appear to be an important indication of how a patient sees herself vis-à-vis her family, whether the family of origin or the patient's current family. The information presented often changes over time. One 56-year-old married patient initially introduced her nuclear family and never discussed or mentioned her family of origin. Her mother was still alive and was significantly involved in her eating disorder. Before the patient entered the program, the mother was sending food packages to the patient and expected a phone call from her daughter every morning. Initially, the patient saw her family situation as very different from the family situations of younger patients and capitalized on her experience as a mother. As she progressed through the program, however, the younger patients indicated that she was apparently still struggling with some of the same parent-child issues that they were. As a result, the patient began to include her mother and sisters in the family introduction and agreed to set up family sessions with her mother.

Although the group is homogeneous in that the patient membership is restricted to those with anorexia nervosa or bulimia nervosa, the family and socioeconomic backgrounds are diverse. Homogeneous groups are best for those persons who can accept and cooperate in treatment by viewing themselves as having problems in common with others and for whom identification provides the strongest medium for self-acceptance and change (Weiner 1982). The homogeneity of patients diagnosed with eating disorders has been a powerful tool with some of the other groups in the program that deal more specifically with the eating disorder. It has been less helpful in the family group because of the members' diverse backgrounds and different life stages. The example of the 56-year-old patient illustrates this. Consequently, we must be more flexible in accepting differences among group members.

One difference that has not been a problem is the inclusion of male patients in the group. In fact, male patients are helpful in defusing some of the stereotypical ideas that patients with eating disorders have about gender influences on power relationships in their families.

Group Structure

History

Several factors were considered in determining the structure and content of the group. There was concern that a too-unstructured group might become a free-for-all, with patients unloading feelings of blame and guilt involving family members. This free-for-all might leave the patients feeling overwhelmed, as if they had experienced a "verbal binge." Other patients might feel that they come from a "perfect" family or a family that protects its members (Root et al. 1986). Therefore, they would naturally feel uncomfortable talking about negative issues. In addition, if the group was open-ended, new members might feel left out.

Considering these factors, it was felt that a more structured psychoeducational model would be most helpful. This model would combine an educational component with discussion and exercises that would explore how family issues affect patients' eating and feelings about themselves. It was decided that the educational aspects of the group would be carried out using themes based on normal family functioning. These themes (discussed in the next section) were collected in writing and handed out to group members, who would then discuss the themes with reference to themselves. It was felt that the themes would help reduce family issues into more understandable and workable parts and provide structure to a topic that is often unclear and chaotic.

Current Model

The family relations group currently has a problem-solving framework that stresses both cognitive and behavioral change. Cognitive change is facilitated by handouts based on specific themes, which help patients look at family myths and expectations more realistically. For example, one handout looks at the family life-cycle as a natural growth process:

> All families and individuals experience changes and stress as they go through the family life-cycle. The cycle is a circular process with an arbitrary beginning and ending. The stages include: the unattached young adult, newly married couple, family with young children, family with adolescents, launching children, family in later life. (Carter and McGoldrick 1980)

The handout helps to normalize the change process by which many of the patients feel threatened. They are not certain why life is not the way it was when they were 12 years old. Patients are encouraged to process their own concerns about feeling "stuck" and what has made it difficult to move on.

The handout also goes into detail about what changes need to take place at each stage. It addresses some of the behavioral changes that are needed to move on to the next stage. Patients may be given homework or assignments to be completed during the next family session. One example involved a 30-year-old single woman who felt that she never left home, although she was living and working in a different city from her family of origin. The patient had been living out of her family's house off and on for 10 years. She still used her parents' address on all of her identification, including her driver's license and credit cards, and all of her mail was delivered to her parents' house. When her driver's license had to be renewed, she asked her family if she should change the address to her current one. She was told no. In the group, the group members suggested that for her to be an unattached adult, she needed to change her identification to reflect her current home address. Reluctantly, she agreed, and she made the changes during the next 2 weeks. She was also given some suggestions about how she could still feel part of her family.

We encourage the group not to explore the patient's history, because this exploration tends to be very frustrating. Patients already talk a great deal on their own about "old material," and this inhibits their ability to move on to new experiences. As a result, current issues are emphasized.

Themes

The content of the group involves eight themes. In choosing themes, we examined the literature on family therapy and theory. Of particular significance are Satir's (1972) communication styles, Minuchin's (1974) family structure, the McMaster model of family functioning (Epstein et al. 1978), the Process model of family functioning (Steinhauer et al. 1984), and the family life-cycle (Carter and McGoldrick 1980). The themes include the following topics:

1. Role of the family
2. Family life-cycle
3. Family roles
4. Communication styles in the family
5. Disagreement and conflict resolution
6. Autonomy and separation
7. Role of food and importance of appearance in the family
8. Role of pets in the family

As these topics indicate, the themes deal with general areas of family functioning, with only one theme specifically addressing food and dieting. The order of presentation of the themes is often determined by group events or specific calendar events such as significant holidays. Most themes are dealt with in no more than 1 or 2 weeks, so new members do not feel as though they are coming into the middle of a group process.

The *role of the family* discussions focus on the structure and function of family units. Borrowing from Minuchin's (1974) structural theory, the handout for this topic states that "the role of the family is to maintain stability while promoting change and growth." In other words, growth and change are not "bad," although many patients and their families feel threatened by change. The *family life-cycle*, which was discussed before, helps patients to understand and normalize the process of change in families.

The *family roles* discussions address traditional and idiosyncratic roles in families and how the two differ. Some patients view their role of mediator or scapegoat as traditional and do not recognize that they have assumed this position for other reasons. Another role to which patients refer is the sick role. This role, particularly if it has been chronic, may have been very significant in a family if the illness and its symptoms have acquired new significance as a regulator in the family system (Minuchin et al. 1978). In addition to the description of traditional and idiosyncratic roles, we have included the issues of values, culture (Steinhauer et al. 1984), and religion and how they affect role acquisition and beliefs—for example, the differences between growing up in a family with an ethnic Italian background and growing up in a Canadian family with an Anglo-Saxon background. The roles and expectations of each family and cultural group will be different.

Discussions of *communication styles* highlight Satir's (1972) placater, blamer, computer, distractor, and leveler styles. Patients are helped to look at how constant stress in their families can make family members feel defensive, resulting in ineffective communication patterns. We stress that ineffective communication styles are forms of hiding or concealing feelings. Leveling is the ideal way of expressing oneself, and through exercises the members try out different ways to level.

Discussion of *disagreement and conflict resolution* helps patients use information received about communication styles. Open disagreement among family members is viewed by most patients as "bad"; consequently, there is a lack of conflict resolution. For some patients, their illness may be viewed as a way of resolving conflict between other family members, since attention is diverted from other issues. This theme helps patients to look at ways in which disagreement could be encouraged (through leveling) and to examine steps to ensure more successful conflict resolution.

The theme of *autonomy and separation* surfaces during discussion of many other topics. Patients living outside their parents' homes often state initially that they are completely autonomous. Yet, it is not unusual for these patients to feel "locked in to" their families. In a handout, autonomy is defined as the feeling of being a separate person who can make her own choices and assume responsibility for those choices. Patients are encouraged to look at themselves with this definition in mind. The difference between physical and emotional separation is emphasized, as are "appropriate separation" and "feeling cut off."

The *role of food and importance of appearance in the family* is a theme that specifically relates to family eating patterns, family expectations regarding looks, and how these patterns and expectations may perpetuate the eating disorder. A handout for this theme includes an examination of the important issues of appearance and food based on whether the family is "Americanized," has a strong ethnic identity, or is "mixed" (Schwartz et al. 1985). The Americanized family tends to place importance on appearing stylish and attractive (which may mean looking thin). In ethnic families, thinness may not be emphasized as much. Indeed, a mother's importance to an ethnic family is often defined by how well her family eats. In mixed families, some family members maintain ethnic values and others adopt Americanized values.

This topic is very important for patients. We often present it at significant meal events, such as occur at Christmas, Thanksgiving, or the Jewish New Year. Patients are generally anxious about eating in front of family members at these times. A patient can be particularly anxious if her mother has spent several days cooking and takes pride in seeing her hard work consumed.

The *role of pets in the family* was not one of the original themes. This topic emerged from a discussion by patients about their pets. Almost 90% of our patients own or have owned a pet. Some patients have included their pets in the family introductions. This session looks at the benefits and drawbacks of pet ownership. A handout for this session states that even though pet ownership can decrease depression and loneliness (Levinson 1972), some studies show that pet owners show a greater liking for pets than for people (Cameron and Mattison 1972).

Many patients talk about the unconditional love they receive from their pet and the need for such a relationship because they do not get this from members of their families. Patients are encouraged to discuss their pets and how they have helped their relationships with others. Interestingly, some patients have noted that, as they gain weight, they feed their pets more.

Techniques

We use numerous techniques to facilitate learning. The techniques include handouts, games (such as a string exercise), videotaping, homework, sculpting, and role playing.

Written handouts seem to help patients understand the family topic from a more objective standpoint. A patient is thus able, through both discussion and experiential exercises, to look at a theme and make specific references to her own situation. We find that nonverbal or action-oriented techniques help those patients who find it difficult to visualize concepts being discussed and may have significant problems expressing feelings. Such techniques also provide a break from most of the other groups in the DHP, which are primarily verbal.

The string exercise helps to illustrate the family life-cycle. It begins with two group members (representing a couple) holding opposite ends of two strings of different colors. The couple is told that each string represents the relationship that each person has with the person holding the opposite end. Group members are instructed that they control only the string that represents their relationship with another individual and can negotiate it in any way they wish. The couple then proceeds through specific life events, such as marriage, children, friendships, adolescents, and death of a parent. As new group members join the exercise, each brings her own string. The complexity of family relationships soon becomes apparent. It has been interesting to observe how the string families created by group members often resemble the families of some of the group members. The exercise can last as long as 1 hour and is then discussed by the group.

Another useful technique is recording sessions on videotape. We have periodically taped our groups, particularly those that involve a role-playing sequence or the string exercise. The tape is played for the group the week after the group has given its impressions of the exercise. Group members find the feedback interesting but difficult. Initially, they are concerned with how they look, particularly if they knew that they had gained weight that week. We have had patients agree to be taped but then refuse to watch the tape because of such concern. Many patients look at the process and are surprised at how different the exercise and feedback appear from the week before. Yalom (1975) stated, "Although feedback about our behavior is important, it is not as convincing as information we discover ourselves; videotape provides feedback which is not mediated through a second person" (p. 438).

Homework is quite important. We often assign homework at the end of group sessions. The tasks facilitate behavioral change and give clear directives to patients. A homework assignment may be a pen-and-paper task, such as writing descriptions of various family roles, or it may be a request for a patient to look for family photographs to bring to the group. The assignment may be to change behavior at a family event, such as staying at the dinner table instead of running upstairs or outside after a meal. For such an assignment, the patient would bring back to the group her impressions of how her changed behavior was perceived by others and how she felt about it.

The final two techniques, sculpting and role playing, have been very useful in our group. Role playing has been commonly used in groups whose patients invent a situation. We have found it helpful for the patients to try real family situations, such as a holiday family meal. Usually the patient whose family is being depicted is asked to direct the sequence with someone else playing her role, thus giving the patient a more objective perspective on her family situation. The sequence includes two scenarios—one presenting the current status of the family and another changing the patient's behavior. One role-playing session occurred during a discussion of Thanksgiving. One bulimic patient described the family scenario at Thanksgiving and assigned family roles to the group members. Her particular concern was how to feel less guilty during this meal, which her mother spent 2 weeks preparing. She felt that it was a family expectation to eat lots of food and that it was her particular role to please her mother. In the description of the mother's role, the group member playing the mother was to remain standing, without eating, throughout the meal. Apparently, this mother never ate what she prepared, especially for special dinners; she would usually eat leftovers from the day before.

The group quickly realized that the patient's guilt was a response to the mother's problem. The group member playing the patient decided to say "no, thank you" in response to the mother's suggestion that the patient take a second helping of food. The patient commented that she was initially upset about the response, because she could never see herself doing that. The group member playing the patient then went on to say that she would prefer eating a family meal with all family members present, including the mother. Everyone stopped eating, and the group member playing the mother quickly sat down. At that point, the others resumed eating.

Although all role-playing sequences are not so dramatic, the impact of these exercises is powerful. The patient whom we just described did follow the group's suggestions, and she felt more in control at meals.

Sculpting, like role playing, provides a three-dimensional view of a situation; however, it is nonverbal. Unlike family sculpting, whereby family members position themselves in a tableau that depicts emotional closeness or distance (Papp et al. 1973), group sculpting has a patient positioning group members to form her family. The group then helps the patient reposition herself to see what happens to her and to other family members. We often use this technique to help illustrate family roles.

Styles of Leadership

The group is led by two therapists—one male and one female as this chapter was being written. This situation was not deliberately planned, but there have been some advantages to it. Patients seem to look to the male leader when issues of fathers, boyfriends, or spouses are discussed. It is almost as if the patients are playing out their feelings with the male figure. In addition, the male/female leadership may resemble a "good" family, headed by a mother and a father. This naturally has led to some ambivalent feelings about what is "good."

The mother/father theme became apparent during one discussion of roles. One male patient was sitting between the two leaders, looking quite uncomfortable. When questioned about this, he admitted that he always tried to be in the middle of his mother and father. At that point, he jumped up and made the male therapist switch chairs so that the "mother" and "father" would be together again. He stated, "I do not want to be responsible for the separation here."

The leaders use various styles and behavior within the group. Depending on the group, the leaders may start off with a more didactic style to introduce a theme. For example, a handout may first be discussed quite objectively. If group members do not understand the concept, the leaders try to explain it further, perhaps using a blackboard.

The leaders also spend much time clarifying, interpreting, and translating feelings and experiences into ideas. Yalom (1975) referred to this as "meaning attribution." This leadership function is extremely important. We feel that patients need assistance in shifting from a feeling level, which seems to keep them "stuck," to an action level. Some group members have had extensive psychotherapy and can give elaborate interpretations of their family dynamics, without changing.

Finally, the leaders are task-oriented. That is, they set the limits, guide the discussion, and direct patients through the various techniques and homework.

Problems

We feel that the family relations group is unique. Its design was intended to deal with some of the problems that exist when a group is part of a larger structure, such as the DHP. As in any therapeutic relationship, however, there are potential therapeutic snares. Some of these snares have been addressed and changed, but other patient-oriented problems continue.

Patient-Oriented Problems

One patient-oriented problem is the staggered admissions and discharges that result in an open-ended group. This problem produces groups of patients at various stages in the treatment process. Various themes are used to avoid a beginning and an end to the group process. For the most part, this format has been helpful. Nevertheless, it is also apparent that patients who have been at the DHP longer seem to be able to integrate the content more than the newer members. At times, patients may request that topics be repeated.

A second concern is the size of the group. Again, this is determined by the number of admissions to the DHP. We find that as the group approaches 12, the members receive less individual time. Attempts have been made to be flexible in increasing the length of time devoted to a theme—to 3 weeks if necessary. Such an increase, however, limits the number of themes covered during an average admission.

Third, the use of various techniques could be seen as a replacement for interpersonal exploration. The techniques are meant to be used as a tool, not as a replacement for group and individual learning. In a study on encounter groups (Lieberman et al. 1973), leaders who used many exercises were popular with their group, but those group members experienced significantly worse outcomes than did members of groups that used few exercises.

Therapist-Oriented Problems

The first therapist-oriented problem is the use of handouts. It is clear that excessive use of handouts could support intellectualization. The handouts are used only as a stepping-stone. Patients are strongly encouraged to personalize the themes and get away from the theory.

Second, leaders who prescribe structured exercises run the risk of establishing norms that could hamper the development of the group (Yalom 1975). Group members may begin to feel that help comes only from the leader and, consequently, will wait their turn. This has been a concern, because patients are often members of other groups that are more structured than the family relations group. Sometimes patients expect the leaders to work with each group member individually, and these patients do not respond to or work with their colleagues directly. Consequently, group members are encouraged to carry out or direct the exercises as much as possible.

Finally, the transition from the family therapy sessions to the family group could present problems concerning secrets and confidentiality. Since the family group leaders are also the family therapists, information about the family and the patient comes from two sources. Often there are significant differences between the way in which families describe themselves in family sessions and the way in which the patient describes the family in the patient group setting. The family therapist/leader knows what has been said in other contexts but may feel concerned about discrepancies, particularly if patients in a group or family members are trying to work with only partial information. Selvini-Palazzoli and Prata (1982) referred to secrets as a major snare in family therapy. The patient knows that the therapist knows differently, but the therapist is unable to tell either the group or the family about discrepancies made by the patient. Accepting a secret from a patient in either setting may mean accepting a coalition with the patient who offers the revelation. Thus, the family therapist/leader could feel stuck, and this increases the possibility of a psychological split or a decrease in the effectiveness of family intervention.

Patients are encouraged to talk about their family sessions in other groups, so the patients already have access to the same knowledge the therapists have. In addition, leaders may question a patient directly in the family group when it is necessary to clarify discrepancies. Patients are usually informed at the first group meeting that information from various groups and family and individual sessions need to be shared so that patients may benefit from the group process. By keeping open communication as a group norm, secrets have been less of a problem than we initially anticipated.

Summary

In this chapter, we review the development and structure of a group focusing on family relationships in the setting of a DHP for treating eating disorders. One of the most interesting results of this group is the increased integration of issues from the family relations group with those from a family therapy group. Initially, family therapists were timid about bringing the two groups together. This integration, however, has been quite useful and at times expedient. In some instances, patients have been coaxed by their peers to pursue an issue in the family therapy session, with the expectation that the patient will then report back to the family relations group.

This group is a valuable adjunct for integrating family involvement and for the consideration of family issues in a program for adults with eating disorders.

References

Bell JE: Family group therapy (Public Health Monograph No 64). Washington, DC, U.S. Government Printing Office, 1961

Bell JE: A theoretical framework for family group therapy, in Family Therapy: Theory and Practice. Edited by Guerin PJ. New York, Gardner, 1976, pp 129–143

Cameron P, Mattison M: Psychological correlates of pet ownership. Psychol Rep 30:286, 1972

Carter EA, McGoldrick M: The family life cycle and family therapy: an overview, in The Family Life Cycle: A Framework for Family Therapy. Edited by Carter EA, McGoldrick M. New York, Gardner, 1980, pp 3–20

Dreikurs R: Family group therapy in the Chicago community child guidance centres. Mental Hygiene 35:291–301, 1951

Epstein NB, Bishop DS, Levin S: The McMaster model of family functioning. Journal of Marriage and Family Counselling 4:19–31, 1978

Garfinkel PE, Garner DM: Anorexia Nervosa: A Multidimensional Perspective. New York, Brunner/Mazel, 1982

Gritzer PH, Okun HS: Multiple family group therapy: a model for all families, in Handbook of Family and Marital Therapy. Edited by Wolman BB, Stricker G. New York, Plenum, 1983, pp 315–342

Levinson B: Pets and Human Development. Springfield, IL, Charles C Thomas, 1972

Lieberman MA, Yalom I, Miles M: Encounter Groups: First Facts. New York, Basic Books, 1973

Minuchin S: Families and Family Therapy. Cambridge, MA, Harvard University Press, 1974

Minuchin S, Rosman B, Baker L: Psychosomatic Families: Anorexia Nervosa in Context. Cambridge, MA, Harvard University Press, 1978

Papp P, Silverstein O, Carter E: Family sculpting in preventive work with well families. Fam Process 12:197–212, 1973

Root MPP, Fallon PF, Friedrich WN: Bulimia: A Systems Approach to Treatment. New York, WW Norton, 1986

Satir V: Peoplemaking. Palo Alto, CA, Science & Behavior Books, 1972

Schwartz RC, Barrett M, Saba G: Family therapy for bulimia, in Handbook of Psychotherapy for Anorexia Nervosa and Bulimia. Edited by Garner DM, Garfinkel PE. New York, Guilford, 1985, pp 280–310

Selvini-Palazzoli M, Prata G: Snares in family therapy. Journal of Marital and Family Therapy 8:4, 1982

Steinhauer PD, Santa-Barbara J, Skinner H: The process model of family functioning. Can J Psychiatry 29:77–88, 1984

Strelnick AH: Multiple family group therapy: a review of the literature. Fam Process 16:307–325, 1977

Weiner MF: Identification in psychotherapy. Am J Psychother 36:109–116, 1982

Wooley SC, Lewis KG: Multi-family therapy within an intensive treatment program for bulimia, in The Family Therapy Collection. Edited by Harkaway JE. Rockville, MD, Aspen, 1987, pp 12–23

Yalom ID: The Theory and Practice of Group Psychotherapy. New York, Basic Books, 1975

Chapter 7

Integrating Individual and Family Therapy in an Inpatient Eating Disorders Unit

LORIE SHEKTER-WOLFSON, M.S.W., C.S.W.
SIDNEY KENNEDY, M.B., F.R.C.P.(C)

Chapter 7

Integrating Individual and Family Therapy in an Inpatient Eating Disorders Unit

*I*t is now generally recognized that a multidimensional approach is required in managing patients with anorexia nervosa (AN) and bulimia nervosa (BN) (Garfinkel and Garner 1982). Family therapy is an important aspect of such treatment for many patients with eating disorders (Hall 1987; Vandereycken 1985). In one of the few controlled treatment trials involving family therapy and eating disorders, Russell et al. (1987) compared family therapy to individual supportive psychotherapy in AN patients after discharge from the hospital. Family therapy was most likely to be associated with a good outcome after 1 year in those patients whose illness began at an early age and had not become chronic. Nevertheless, there is still a paucity of controlled trials of family treatment for AN and BN.

Numerous authors have addressed practical issues related to the treatment of such families (Sargent et al. 1985; Wooley and Lewis 1987) and formulated theoretical rationales for particular interventions (Minuchin et al. 1978; Roberto 1986; Schwartz et al. 1985; Selvini-Palazzoli 1978; White 1987). As multidimensional, integrated treatment programs have become more the norm, family therapists have had to learn to integrate individual and family therapies, modalities once thought to be incompatible (McDermott and Charr 1974).

In this chapter, we focus on some of the theoretical and practical issues that arise when individual and family treatments are integrated in an inpatient eating disorders unit. Since the majority of patients with AN and BN are female, patients are referred to as *she*. This should not suggest that males cannot develop an eating disorder.

Early schools of psychotherapeutic thought emphasized the primacy of intrapsychic phenomena, and many of these models discouraged contact with family members. Nichols (1984) commented on the discrepancy inherent in early psychoanalytic thought between the putative etiologic agents of psychological distress and the proposed treatment. In these models, psychological illness was thought to have arisen because of dysfunctional interactions between the "patient" and other people in his or her environment, usually including family. Ironically, the therapy proposed for such disorders simply walled off the identified patient from these supposedly noxious influences.

Despite this paradox, the interaction between the clinical status of the patient and his or her environment had long been recognized and was graphically illustrated in a case description by Jackson (1954). In this case, he was treating a depressed woman. As she began to improve, her husband called to say that his emotional condition had deteriorated. As she improved further, the husband lost his job and eventually committed suicide.

The development of systemic ways of understanding families produced marked changes in the way in which the patient's problem was viewed. These changes included a fundamental redefinition of personality development, abnormal behavior, and treatment (Nichols 1984). Whereas the individual therapist viewed the symptom as a result of an intrapsychic process, the family therapist began to view it as a result of an interpersonal process. Differences in theoretical orientation elicited a dichotomous approach to treatment, with the patient being treated either alone or as a member of a family system. Initially, it would have been rare to consider a combination of these therapeutic modalities; however, during the last 10 years there have been attempts to integrate the two.

Integrating individual and family therapy has been neither an easy nor an uneventful process (McDermott and Charr 1974). The proponents of each school of therapy have gradually begun to recognize the validity of the other; however, there are few published reports suggesting either guidelines or methodology with only limited work in this area (Steinhauer and Tisdall 1984).

In hospitals using multidisciplinary teams and multidimensional approaches, it is not unusual for patients to be involved in individual, group, and family therapies concurrently. Treatment in such a setting is then focused on different levels of functioning at different times. Vandereycken (1985) commented that "a multidimensional approach requires an integrative way of thinking on the part of the therapist. . . . This is necessary in order to avoid 'unproductive supermarket' treatment."

Steinhauer and Tisdall (1984) offered some ideas of what to expect from the respective therapies and when therapists should refer patients to concurrent family and individual therapy. The role of the family therapist includes helping family members begin to separate and accept responsibility for their own behavior. The role of the individual therapist is to help the family member identify and resolve conflicts interfering with the development of autonomy.

A family therapist should consider making a referral for individual therapy when one family member repeatedly dominates sessions or when a family member lacks adequate impulse control to tolerate sessions. An individual therapist should consider a referral when an individual is preoccupied with marital or family disturbance or when progress in the individual therapy is disrupting the family equilibrium to an unmanageable degree.

Although these guidelines are helpful in understanding the limitations of each particular modality, it is important to recognize that concurrent family and individual treatment is not necessary in each case.

The Inpatient Treatment Setting for Eating Disorders

The inpatient eating disorders unit at the Toronto General Hospital has been in operation since 1982 as a five-bed unit in a general psychiatric service. Patients are all 18 years of age or older. The majority of patients have a DSM-III-R (American Psychiatric Association 1987) diagnosis of AN, with or without BN, and a few have BN only (Kennedy and Garfinkel 1989). Ninety-five percent of the patients have been female.

The multidisciplinary team consists of a psychiatrist, a psychiatric resident, a psychologist, a social worker, an occupational therapist, a nutritionist, and a nursing staff. Treatment is multidimensional; its goals are nutritional rehabilitation, disengagement from families, and encouraging patients to develop more constructive ways of expressing autonomy (Kerr and Kennedy 1986; Stern et al. 1981).

Nutritional rehabilitation is achieved by a noncoercive behavioral program in which privileges are determined by progress in terms of weight. A discharge weight is set in consultation with the patient. Patients spend an increasing amount of time outside the hospital as they proceed through the program, in an attempt to promote application of what was learned in the hospital to the outside environment.

Nutritional rehabilitation may have a different meaning for the bulimic patient. Weight gain may not be as much of an issue as regular eating and the cessation of binge eating and purging.

Individual therapy is carried out by the psychiatric resident or psychologist. This is usually limited to one or two sessions per week, often focusing on issues of individuation and separation. The nursing staff also sees patients on a regular basis, providing support and assistance in normalizing eating.

Group therapies, led by the occupational therapist and nutritionist, include food-related groups—such as meal-preparation and nutrition groups—and groups addressing assertion, skill acquisition, and anger control.

Family therapy is an important part of the overall treatment, regardless of a patient's living situation. The focus of family sessions is to aid families with the issues of separation and autonomy and to help families adjust during the recovery process. Family sessions usually start soon after a patient's admission to the hospital.

Patient-family visits are initially restricted to 2 hours on the weekends until the patient's eating is under some control. It is felt that patients must set some limit to time spent with their families, but they may be unable to do this on their own when starved and cognitively impaired. Problems with boundaries are common, and a period of separation may be beneficial, especially at the beginning of treatment, when eating is most out of control. This early period of treatment, with external controls, is similar to Winnicott's (1965) description of the holding environment.

For some parents, admitting a child to the hospital is a sign of failure. Such an attitude may result in the patient receiving overt or covert messages not to "connect" with the treatment team. If this is the case, extensive contact between the family and the patient may be problematic in the early stages of treatment (Stern et al. 1981). The length of admission varies and is significantly affected by the patient's diagnosis. Patients with AN stay an average of 12 weeks; patients with BN only are usually admitted for a time-limited period of 6 weeks.

Integrating Individual and Family Therapies

The integration of individual and family therapies involves four areas: 1) balancing individual and family therapies; 2) the family's acceptance of family-oriented treatment; 3) the involvement of the patient in concurrent individual psychotherapy; and 4) termination and discharge planning issues.

Balancing Individual and Family Therapies

Family involvement may appear confusing at first to the patient and her family, because it is the patient who has been hospitalized and designated as the "problem." From a purely systems perspective, the eating disorder is viewed either as a symptom of dysfunctional family structure or as the identified patient's response to an impossibly confusing situation for which the family's solution has become a problem itself (Watzlawick et al. 1974).

If the family therapist's task is to help establish appropriate boundaries and hierarchies within the family system, the patient must be helped with issues of separation and autonomy. This may appear contradictory to the patient and family when the patient is initially placed on bed rest with her bathroom locked and her meals supervised. Family members may also be reluctant to give up their shared preoccupation with food intake and weight and accept that this is now a matter for the patient and treatment team to handle.

The first task of the family therapist is to create a new therapeutic system that will involve not only the staff and the patient, but the family as well (Sargent et al. 1985). Underlying this task is the assumption that, when the patient is hospitalized, the family is indirectly hospitalized as well.

Many of the family's struggles with the patient may be replicated with the hospital staff. While the patient is receiving individual help with her struggles, the family therapist needs to be aware of the complementary struggle of the family. The family may approach the team with mixed reactions—wanting to be helped but also wanting to direct the helping process.

Family therapists need to have therapist maneuverability (Fisch et al. 1983). Some families threaten to sabotage the treatment from the outset, usually by setting conditions for treatment that limit the therapist's freedom to maneuver constructively. The therapist must be clear about the ground rules for treatment without excessively exerting his or her authority.

Stern et al. (1981) described the early stage of therapy in such a setting as similar to Winnicott's (1965) "battle for structure." This battle involves the family testing the therapist or the therapeutic team to see whether they are strong enough to maintain authority over and control of the therapeutic structure. If the therapist cannot exert effective leadership and direction in the initial stages of therapy, he or she can hardly be trusted to ensure safety and constructive work should additional issues surface.

This need to establish control of the therapeutic situation while encouraging familial autonomy and responsibility is a delicate balancing act. In the middle of all of this activity is the patient, who is concurrently engaged in a parallel struggle with her "treatment family." The nuclear family, including the patient, must therefore be part of the initial decision-making process. Specific issues such as weighing the patient, setting meal plans, and meal supervision are the responsibility of the treatment team, and families should be discouraged from getting involved in these issues. This symptom separation is helpful in teaching families to set more appropriate boundaries. The degree to which a family is able to disengage from the symptom may be an indication of the degree of rigidity and enmeshment present in the family (Schwartz et al. 1985).

To help the family with symptom separation, the therapist must have rapport with both the patient and the family. An example of this type of intervention would be the following:

> It seems important for this family to know the patient's weight from week to week; however, your daughter's weight is like a barometer. If her weight goes down, everyone seems sad and depressed. If her weight

goes up, everyone is glad. Let us see what other situations change the feelings of the family.

The controlled nature of the inpatient hospital setting can also create difficulties for extrasessional homework tasks. The patient, who is in the hospital, has access to team members to help her review family sessions and rehearse new strategies, whereas the family may feel "left out." Some authors have advocated admitting the whole family to deal with this problem (Portner 1977), but this is not practical in our setting.

The technique of enactment, as described by Minuchin and Fishman (1981), may be another way of addressing the issue of getting the family more involved in the therapeutic process. Minuchin and Fishman feel that family members try to explain or discuss problems using a one-dimensional perspective. When the therapist encourages family members to interact, sequences beyond the family's control are unleashed. This is referred to as the "family dance." Encouraging such family interactions in the protected setting of the family session will help the family understand what the changes in the family are going to be like for the family.

One way to induce the family dance is to arrange a lunch session. Lunch sessions in the inpatient unit are somewhat different from those described by Minuchin et al. (1978), whose goal was to transform the issue of one anorexic patient into the drama of a dysfunctional family. Rather than introduce such sessions at the beginning of treatment, when the patient's eating is at its most disturbed, it is usually more helpful to wait until the patient's eating behavior is under control. The focus of these sessions is to help the patient generalize some of the learning from the protected setting of the inpatient unit and apply it to a more realistic situation. The lunch session is carried out with the family if the patient is returning home or with a boyfriend or spouse if this is appropriate.

In one case, the patient (aged 25) had the most difficulty eating with her father. Her parents had been separated for several years and she was still living with her mother, so most of their meals were taken in restaurants. Therefore, a restaurant seemed to be a natural lunch setting.

The first stage was to invite the father for a meal in the hospital cafeteria. A second meal was arranged in a restaurant, with the family therapist in attendance to help the patient and her father with their difficulties talking in this environment. These two earlier sessions allowed the patient and her father to eat alone on a third attempt.

Timing of Family Therapy and the Family's Acceptance of Family-Oriented Treatment

The nutritional status of a patient may affect the timing of family therapy. Psychological therapies are unlikely to be mutative in the face of the cognitive effects of starvation. These effects were reviewed by Kaplan and Woodside (1987). It is important for family therapists to be aware that bulimic patients at a statistically normal weight may be physiologically starved because of fasting periods or excessive dieting. Both insight-oriented therapy and family therapy may need to be delayed until the patient is more nutritionally stable. Until such time, individual support remains important and should focus on short-term, concrete goals. During this time, it is helpful for the family to have an understanding of what is occurring but not to be involved in family therapy.

The family is usually at its most defensive during the early stages of admission, when the patient is having the most difficulty. The staff must consider not only the readiness of the patient for family work, but the readiness of the family as well. Timing is crucial in helping the family accept the problem and adapt to change.

Vandereycken (1985) discussed the advantages of a family-oriented approach instead of a family therapy approach. A family-oriented approach includes the flexible use of various modalities—educational guidance, counseling, and family therapy if indicated. In the early stages of hospitalization, the family will benefit most from a psychoeducational approach, during which time myths about AN and BN can be debunked and concerns arising from previous failed treatment attempts can be expressed. Useful information can include advice about limit setting or suggestions for reading material.

Other factors that may have to be considered regarding the timing of family involvement include the method of refeeding and the geographic location of the family. If a patient is being fed through a tube, it is very difficult to involve the patient in family therapy, mainly because of the external struggle for control. The sight of the family member being fed through a tube can also be very upsetting for others in the family.

If the patient's family lives far away from the treatment setting, the family may be asked to visit later rather than earlier, especially if the family is only able to visit once or twice. Delaying sessions in this way will reduce the focus on issues of eating and allow other family conflicts to surface. Conference calls may also be helpful when families live some distance from the hospital.

The nature of the presenting symptom will significantly affect the family's acceptance of family involvement. In the case of AN, the patient's obvious weight loss is more likely to have produced open conflict within the family, perhaps including struggles at the dinner table. The situation may be markedly different for BN. If the family has been aware of the bulimic symptoms, open conflict similar to that within the family of an anorexic patient may have developed over the prevention of binge eating or purging. Bulimic symptoms may be more overtly offensive to the family, who view binge eating as "stealing food" and vomiting as "abusing the plumbing." An angry family will be less able to become involved in the therapeutic process.

Bulimic behavior that has been more secretive has different implications for family involvement. Usually, a bulimic patient who has kept her problem to herself is more interested in getting treatment for herself alone than for the family. The family may have been informed of the bulimic symptoms just prior to assessment for treatment or hospitalization. Therefore, the family has not had an opportunity to be involved in the more obvious struggles that may characterize the families of anorexic or openly bulimic patients. Families of "secret" bulimic patients may require greater assistance than other families, particularly in providing accurate information. It is important to appreciate that not only the patients but also the families will come for treatment at different levels of understanding and acceptance.

In the inpatient unit, these various issues are dealt with in several ways. Anorexic patients are often initially assessed without the family present. When family meetings are arranged, it is important to emphasize to the family that the purpose of the sessions is not to attach blame but to reframe the problem as a family issue so that everyone can help to resolve the problem and have an opportunity to address feelings of frustration and helplessness. It is important to address the issue in this way to validate the family's perception of the problem. Families are often comforted by the thesis that no one is to blame for the problem. This comfort allows the family to be involved in the treatment later without constant fear or guilt.

Secret bulimic patients may feel that their families should not be involved, since the disorder has been deliberately hidden from them. A patient will have to be seen individually to address the reasons for the secretiveness and the problems of secrets in general within the family system. During this time, some general information about the eating disorder may help family members begin to understand what has been happening. Family members often concede that they suspected that the patient had an eating problem, but the style of communicating within the family is such that secrets are maintained.

Involvement in Concurrent Family and Individual Therapy

When the inpatient unit was being created, it was generally recognized that family and individual sessions would be occurring concurrently. The unit's staff members agreed that both intrapsychic and interpersonal problems needed to be addressed (Steinhauer and Tisdall 1984). Individual and family treatments offered concurrently rather than as mutually exclusive treatments can come closer than either treatment alone to duplicating, within the therapeutic environment, what patients encounter outside a treatment environment. This is an important theoretical base from which to work, particularly because many patients with eating disorders have such difficulty dealing with the separation phase of the family life-cycle (Bruch 1979). In addition, some patients find it difficult to assert themselves within the family system while trying to increase self-esteem, develop a capacity for trusting relationships, and understand the nature of their symptoms (Garner et al. 1982). In practice, implementing such dual therapy requires mutual understanding of the theoretical bases for each (e.g., the linear model of individual therapy versus the systems model of family therapy) and close teamwork.

In the inpatient unit, a patient is seen twice weekly by the psychiatric resident or psychologist for individual psychotherapy. For a patient who is in the hospital for several months, this can prove to be a very important relationship. Patients are also assigned to a primary nurse-therapist, who is involved in many of the patient's day-to-day activities, such as supervising meals and bed-rest activities and dealing with the frustration the patient may experience while in the unit.

The family therapist rarely sees a patient alone. Most contact is with other family members or other significant people in the patient's life. Because of these different circumstances, different staff members may develop markedly discrepant views of the patient. This divergence can be further intensified when the family therapy moves into the stage that Whittaker (1977) called the "battle for initiative." This is the stage at which families start to take some responsibility for the direction of their treatment. Families of anorexic patients may be experts at displacing responsibility and initiative to others while appearing to comply with external demands (Stern et al. 1981). Family therapists may see such passive noncompliance in a light different from that of individual therapists, and this difference can create a psychological split of the therapeutic team.

The technique of crisis induction in family therapy is another potential cause for a split of the therapeutic team. Minuchin et al. (1978) felt that many families will only be motivated to act differently when their anxiety level is sufficiently high. Models of family therapy advocating crisis induction could be seen as potentially harmful to a patient if not understood by all team members. Consistency among team members about therapeutic decisions is vital. In the inpatient unit, such information is shared during twice-weekly team rounds.

The importance of sharing information regularly among team members cannot be overemphasized. The absence of such sharing may replicate the family system of the patient, in which coalitions are covertly established through the use of secrets. Selvini-Palazzoli and Prata (1982) described secrets as a major snare in family therapy, but this description is also applicable to integrated family and individual therapy. In the inpatient unit, patients and families are informed at the outset of treatment that all information collected by the team is shared by the team.

A case example may illustrate some of these points.

A patient was admitted with a 3-year history of AN. Her parents had divorced 6 years earlier, and an older brother had assumed the role of head of the family. It was thought at the time of the original assessment that the patient's mother was significantly and pathologically involved in her daughter's abnormal eating patterns.

Initially, the patient was quite reluctant to be in the hospital and felt that the admission had been her mother's idea. With some effort, the individual therapist was able to establish a relationship with the patient, who then began to eat.

In the family sessions, the patient's eating seemed to be more related to a wish to be compliant than to a wish to improve. The patient was concerned that she would lose her mother's love and her brother's concern if she were to improve. Her brother initially fought with the staff about most of the program rules, feeling that they were oppressive, and stated his belief that the program was unlikely to lead to his sister's improvement. He felt that he knew what his sister needed much more accurately than did the staff.

The staff felt it was important to help the family understand the treatment without forcing it on the family or the patient. Staff members attempted to help the mother recognize that she was feeling out of control, able to influence neither the staff nor her son. With some assistance, the mother began to take more appropriate control in the treatment plan.

A crisis was induced when the brother was asked not to come to one of the family sessions. The mother made it clear that she would like to take over more parenting functions, because she felt it was no longer her son's role to be a second parent in the family. The patient initially reacted quite angrily to this apparent lack of involvement on the part of her brother, and she briefly returned to her habit of not eating. The rest of the treatment team became quite concerned about what was happening in the family sessions.

Further meetings were scheduled to help the mother take increased initiative in the treatment. When the mother became more effective, the patient began to eat again, thus regaining some control of herself. The brother was eventually invited back to the sessions to talk about the nature of his relationship with his sister and how the relationship could be modified into something more appropriate for a brother and sister. Individual sessions began to center on the patient's role in the family and her concerns about "losing" her mother and brother when she got well.

The high frequency of team meetings allowed us to share information about both the individual and family sessions. This minimized the possibility of the patient keeping secrets and playing one component of the staff off against the other.

Termination and Discharge Planning for the Patient and Family

The timing of discharge is usually a medical decision, related to the patient's ability to achieve and maintain a specific weight or to eat a normal diet without binging or purging. As the time for discharge approaches, plans for housing, schooling, and vocational planning also need to be finalized.

Generally, many of the less-tangible issues, such as separation or conflict resolution in the family, have not been resolved as the discharge nears. This may lead to frustration on the part of the family therapist, who feels that family issues were left unfinished while other eating-related issues were handled. This generally leads to one of two scenarios.

In the first scenario, the patient and the staff may feel that individual therapy as an outpatient is now required. The family therapist may have helped the family system cope with the patient's moves toward separation and individuation, and it is now up to the patient to carry on the process herself. In this situation, a follow-up family session would usually be arranged for about 6 months after discharge.

In the second scenario, ongoing family or marital therapy may be recommended. There are numerous reasons why such a recommendation might be made. In some families, inadequate progress has been made in encouraging the patient to be appropriately autonomous. In other families, specific family subsystems may become more dysfunctional as the patient improves. Crisp et al. (1977) noted marked deteriorations in the marital relationships of parents of restricting anorexic patients during the course of successful treatment, whereas the marital relationships of parents of anorexic and bulimic patients actually improved with successful treatment.

If a patient is married or living in a common-law relationship, couple sessions may need to continue even though sessions with the family of origin are not required. This type of suggestion is useful when the patient feels that work with her new family is more important than older issues with her family of origin. In this situation, the patient would be recognized as having made a major shift in her life-cycle.

Summary

The practical difficulties of integrating family work into the overall structure of an inpatient treatment program are significant. Successful integration requires flexibility in the family therapist and in the rest of the treatment team. Open communication, with clear statements of goals for specific interventions and the likely impact of such interventions, is an important factor in successfully combining treatment modalities. The additional information and perspective gained by all parties through the integration of individual and family therapy enhances the therapeutic efforts of each party.

References

American Psychiatric Association: Diagnostic and Statistical Manual of Mental Disorders, 3rd Edition, Revised. Washington, DC, American Psychiatric Association, 1987

Bruch H: Eating Disorders: Obesity, Anorexia Nervosa, and the Person Within. New York, Basic Books, 1979

Crisp AH, Harding B, McGuinness B: Anorexia nervosa: psychoneurotic characteristics of parents: relationship to prognosis. J Psychosom Res 118:167–173, 1977

Fisch R, Wakeland JH, Segal L: The Tactics of Change: Doing Therapy Briefly. San Francisco, CA, Jossey-Bass, 1983

Garfinkel PE, Garner DM: Anorexia Nervosa: A Multidimensional Perspective. New York, Brunner/Mazel, 1982

Garner DM, Garfinkel PE, Bemis KM: A multidimensional psychotherapy for anorexia nervosa. International Journal of Eating Disorders 1:3–46, 1982

Hall A: The place of family therapy in the treatment of anorexia nervosa. Aust N Z J Psychiatry 21:568–574, 1987

Jackson DD: Suicide. Sci Am 191:88–96, 1954

Kaplan AS, Woodside DB: Biologic aspects of anorexia nervosa and bulimia nervosa. J Clin Consult Psychol 55:645–653, 1987

Kennedy SH, Garfinkel PE: Patients admitted to hospital for anorexia nervosa and bulimia nervosa: psychotherapy, weight gain and attitudes towards treatment. International Journal of Eating Disorders 8:181–190, 1989

Kerr A, Kennedy SH: Inpatient treatment for anorexia nervosa and bulimia nervosa. British Review of Anorexia Nervosa and Bulimia 2:5–16, 1986

McDermott H, Charr WF: The undeclared war between child and family therapy. J Am Acad Child Psychiatry 13:422–436, 1974

Minuchin S, Fishman HC: Family Therapy Techniques. Cambridge, MA, Harvard University Press, 1981

Minuchin S, Rosman BL, Baker L: Psychosomatic Families: Anorexia Nervosa in Context. Cambridge, MA, Harvard University Press, 1978

Nichols M: Family Therapy: Concepts and Methods. New York, Gardner, 1984

Portner DL: Hospitalization of the family in the treatment of anorexia nervosa. Health & Soc Work 2:111–122, 1977

Roberto LG: Bulimia: a transgenerational view. Journal of Marital and Family Therapy 12:231–240, 1986

Russell GFM, Szmukler GI, Dare C, et al: An evaluation of family therapy in anorexia nervosa and bulimia nervosa. Arch Gen Psychiatry 44:1047–1056, 1987

Sargent J, Liebman R, Silver M: Family therapy for anorexia nervosa, in Handbook of Psychotherapy for Anorexia Nervosa and Bulimia. Edited by Garner DM, Garfinkel PE. New York, Guilford, 1985, pp 257–279

Schwartz RC, Barrett ML, Saba G: Family therapy for bulimia, in Handbook of Psychotherapy for Anorexia Nervosa and Bulimia. Edited by Garner DM, Garfinkel PE. New York, Guilford, 1985, pp 280–310

Selvini-Palazzoli M: Self Starvation. New York, Jason Aronson, 1978

Selvini-Palazzoli M, Prata G: Snares in family therapy. Journal of Marital and Family Therapy 8:443–450, 1982

Steinhauer PD, Tisdall GW: The integrated use of individual and family psychotherapy. Can J Psychiatry 29:88–97, 1984

Stern S, Whittaker C, Hagemann N, et al: Anorexia nervosa: the hospital's role in family treatment. Fam Process 20:395–408, 1981

Vandereycken W: Inpatient treatment of anorexia nervosa: some research-guided changes. J Psychiatr Res 19:413–422, 1985

Watzlawick P, Weakland J, Fisch R: Change: Principles of Problem Formation and Problem Resolution. New York, WW Norton, 1974

White M: Anorexia nervosa: a cybernetic approach, in The Family Therapy Collection. Edited by Harkaway JE. Rockville, MD, Aspen, 1987, pp 117–129

Whittaker C: Process techniques of family therapy. Interaction 2:4–19, 1977

Winnicott DW: The Maturational Processes and the Facilitating Environment. London, Hogarth Press, 1965

Wooley SC, Lewis KG: Multi-family therapy within an intensive treatment program for bulimia, in The Family Therapy Collection. Edited by Harkaway JE. Rockville, MD, Aspen, 1987, pp 12–23

Chapter 8

Mutual Support Groups for Families in Management of Eating Disorders

DONNA MacAULAY, M.S.W., C.S.W.

Chapter 8

Mutual Support Groups for Families in Management of Eating Disorders

Mutual support groups for families are a valuable adjunct to services for the management of eating disorders. Many such groups have developed in the last decade in response to the needs of families, friends, and significant others. In this chapter, I attempt to clarify what family support groups are, what forms they have taken, and what their role is in the overall management of patients with eating disorders. This chapter includes information about how to organize or contact such groups, their value to the participants, and the roles that professionals and paraprofessionals can play. The multiple functions that such groups serve and the kinds of activities that can develop are also described.

The rapid and widespread growth of self-help and mutual-aid groups has been a significant development in health care delivery during the last two decades. For the most part, these groups have developed as grass roots phenomena from meetings of people who have shared common interests or faced common problems. There are groups and organizations for physical illness (Alzheimer's Society), for substance-use disorders (Narcanon and Alcoholics Anonymous), and for life-cycle changes (Widow to Widow and Parents Without Partners). There are many self-

143

help and family support groups addressing mental health problems, such as Friends of Schizophrenics and the National Alliance for the Mentally Ill.

There have been three major forces contributing to the growth of mutual self-help groups. The first is the financial constraints placed on the provision of mental health services by third-party payers (governments and insurance companies). As limits on the funding of new treatment programs or limits on reimbursement for existing programs increase, there may be less time available from mental health professionals for the education and support of families of affected individuals.

The second force is the growing sense of consumerism and a questioning of what has been traditionally regarded as expert advice on the treatment of mental disorders. Concomitant to this is the growing recognition of the value of experiential knowledge, which has gone hand in hand with the third force—the growing recognition that families constitute the major source of care for the mentally ill.

Families want and need accurate information about mental health problems, to obtain help and to make informed choices. Studies show that families want to connect with others facing the same problem, but few actually get the opportunity to do so (R. Thompson, D. MacAulay, and S. Weisberg, 1987, unpublished observations).

A lack of support in personal and community networks may contribute to a high demand for family support groups. A family member with a mental health problem may be viewed as being in a "stigmatizing" situation, with family members receiving "courtesy stigma" (Borkman 1984, p. 209). Since the nature of mental illness is often confusing and misunderstood and the affected person's behaviors may appear bizarre, it may be difficult for the usual social networks that families depend on to provide adequate empathic support.

Borkman (1984) defined mutual-aid self-help groups as "voluntary associations of persons with common problems who band together to resolve their difficulties by mutual efforts; they are voluntarily developed and controlled by persons sharing the common problem" (p. 206).

Participation in mutual-aid groups is said to have the potential to change the social support system for families of sufferers (Borkman 1984, pp. 212–314). When there is a decreased level and intensity of support from the usual sources, mutual-aid groups can provide a replacement source of understanding and caring. This process can help a family member become "destigmatized." A family's perspective can then change positively, and new knowledge can be gained and shared. In the process of gaining new skills and helping others, new roles, relationships, and self-esteem are developed.

Family Support Groups in Management of Eating Disorders

The presence of a family member with an eating disorder can have an almost catastrophic effect on a family. The persistent high level of tension during every meal day in and day out can undermine the physical and mental health of parents, siblings, and spouses. Family functioning may be increasingly distorted and individual needs subordinated to the needs of the ill person. Because some individuals suffering from eating disorders appear "normal" in almost every way, family members may feel that others cannot understand their concern and suffering. There may be nothing obviously suspect about the thinking and talking of the individual with the disorder, and she may appear to function very well. This appearance of normalcy may mean that the family encounters resistance from the first professionals to whom they turn for help. Friends and relatives may be sympathetic but skeptical in the face of apparent normalcy juxtaposed with stories about bizarre eating rituals, locked refrigerators, or excessive exercising. The frustration caused by lack of understanding from outside the family is compounded by the frequent and stubborn refusal of the anorexic or bulimic individual to acknowledge that professional intervention is required. Family members may feel even more guilty and isolated when they discover theories in their search for information, implying that families are somehow to blame for the eating problem.

Starting a Family Support Group

Existing organizations have demonstrated that there is a wide range of viable ways to start and maintain family support groups. Some, such as the American Anorexia Nervosa Association in New Jersey, began with a parent and health care professionals forming a board to oversee the development and other functions of the organizations—at local and national levels. Others, such as the Anorexia Bulimia Family Support Group of Metropolitan Toronto, started with a few family members and one health care professional simply finding a public room and advertising the first meeting in community-events columns of local newspapers. Those who attended the first meeting of such a group participated in formulating the organization's goals, and plans were developed about how these goals could be achieved. Local groups may choose to affiliate with a national group as a chapter or decide to remain focused on local issues while informally keeping in touch with groups in other geographic areas.

Existing groups and organizations are, for the most part, generous with advice and printed materials for families wishing to start their own groups. Information about existing groups can be found in several places: local information centers, national self-help clearing houses in Canada and the United States, the Canadian National Eating Disorder Information Centre in Toronto, and the Canadian Mental Health Association.

A new family support group may have a better chance of stability if it begins as a partnership of professionals and family members. It is extremely important, however, that family members have a sense of ownership of the organization. Discussions during the first meetings need to be open so that everyone gets an opportunity to speak. Confidentiality must be emphasized so that all participants feel that they have a safe place to express themselves.

In the early stages, the group can be supported financially by "passing the hat" at meetings. Eventually, there are advantages to either incorporating and then obtaining a charitable tax status or requesting that the local mental health association receive tax-receipted contributions to the organization. Most, if not all, groups are supported by memberships and donations.

A steering committee is the minimum structure initially required to ensure that support and information groups meet on a regular basis. Further services will require that a board or several other committees be formed. Some of the committees can be

1. A welcoming committee to take responsibility for introducing new members into the group and its activities
2. An educational committee to arrange for speakers and to gather new information about treatment and research
3. A book or publication committee to review new books and to publish guidelines for parents
4. A communications committee to inform members about events, publish a newsletter, or communicate with other groups
5. A telephone-line committee
6. A fund-raising or finance committee

Some organizations are elaborate enough to have an office and staff. Some have organized successful conferences, workshops, and awareness events. Mutual support groups for the management of eating disorders are almost invariably supportive of professional treatment for eating disorders. Group members can play a crucial role in advocating new or expanded treatment facilities and can lobby various levels of government and funding agencies. At times, members of support groups may sit on advisory boards of treatment facilities or hospitals.

If a group is large enough, there are strong reasons to consider incorporation, a constitution, and a more formal organizational structure. Such formal structures ensure stability and continuity when leaders or members are burned out or unable to continue. These structures provide a mechanism for new members to assume leadership roles and for others to relinquish their roles when their personal lives or inclinations make that necessary.

Purposes of Family Support Groups for Management of Eating Disorders

Most mutual-aid groups for the management of eating disorders are organized by family members and professionals for the following specific reasons:

1. To provide mutual support in a confidential atmosphere for family members in similar situations
2. To learn techniques for coping with a disorder
3. To gather information about research and available treatment resources
4. To advocate increased public awareness and more comprehensive treatment programs

Mutual Support

Mutual support is the core function of any family support group. Although the effects of participating in a mutual support group are often therapeutic, the effects are clearly distinct from group therapy. The major goal of the group is to give and receive help and support. To allow this, the group needs to be led in a relatively nondirective manner by parents or by parents and health care professionals.

Support groups must be structured for the needs of the participants.

Thus, an anorexic or bulimic individual will benefit most from her own peer support group, which is best run by a health care professional in tandem with a recovered anorexic or bulimic patient. Families and friends will participate in a family support group. Although family support groups are composed mainly of parents and siblings, the needs of spouses, lovers, and friends of individuals with eating disorders also need to be acknowledged and addressed. At some meetings, groups may want to divide into smaller groups of those family members who are coping with an anorexic individual and those who are coping with a bulimic individual.

The major reason why individuals with eating disorders should be in one group and family members in another is to allow the members of each group the freedom to express their fears and frustrations without feeling that they are directly criticizing others in their family.

At times, family groups will wish to hear what the experience is like for the sufferer and vice versa. One way to accomplish this is to invite a recovered anorexic patient to speak at a meeting. Another way to accomplish this is to have several family groups meet simultaneously one evening, with patients attending groups that do not contain members of their own families. Thus, objective sharing from the two sides of living with the illness and living with a person who has the illness can occur. Family groups are often attended by individuals with a hidden or unacknowledged eating disorder; this experience can help such individuals recognize the illness and seek treatment.

When family members first come to a support group, they are confronted with two realities: 1) the prolonged nature of the illness and the treatment process; and 2) hope provided by family members who have survived their own situations, and are able to share support and tales of some successes with newcomers.

Becoming aware of the length of the illness-recovery process can be a devastating experience. This may be counterbalanced by a sense of relief at having one's situation finally understood by others. Family members occasionally come to support groups looking for information about the ultimate expert or cure. By hearing others' stories, they realize that there are no miracles but there are many individual ways of making progress toward either recovery from or appropriate adaption to a chronic illness.

Many family members feel that they have no choice but to be dependent on experts and health care professionals because of the complex nature of these illnesses and the frightening and potentially lethal complications that can occur. At times, they may vent considerable anger toward health care professionals. A health care professional involved with a support group needs to be aware that this anger is natural and to understand that these angry parents very much want to believe that the experts will neither fail them nor blame them.

Learning and Sharing Skills for Coping With the Disorder

In many cultures, parents are held responsible for their children's successes or problems. Parents usually do not have a health care professional's sophisticated understanding of theories of family interaction. Parents may react to their own perception of blame by seeking genetic and physiological etiologies for an illness. By sharing accurate knowledge and well-thought-out guidelines for helping an anorexic or bulimic individual, a support group gradually enables its participants to shed some of the guilt that they may feel while taking responsibility for changing patterns that are inadvertently perpetuating disordered eating behavior. Participating in a support group may enable family members to consider the need for family therapy if this is appropriate. Families need both knowledge and empathic support, however, to feel safe enough to think about making changes.

As long as a nonjudgmental, nonblaming atmosphere is maintained along with mutual support, parents and other family members can learn guidelines from others about what works and what does not work in living with an individual with an eating disorder. Such guidelines have been passed along through groups in North America. These include loving the person with the disorder, avoiding comparing him or her to others, encouraging his or her independence and autonomy, and trusting him or her to develop his or her own values and standards. Group members can support each other in not policing or discussing food intake. They can support each other in tolerating physical separation from the individual with the disorder when necessary. They can help each other to reinvolve themselves with their other children and to revive interest in their own and their partners' individual needs. Such advice is more acceptable when it comes from other parents who obviously love their children. (These guidelines are loosely based on a set of guidelines developed by a group of parents in Troy, New York.)

Gathering Information About Research and Available Treatment Resources

Families, in their need for information, must learn about multidimensional causation and treatment. This can be achieved by inviting speakers to meetings on a regular basis, such as hospital-based health care professionals and private practitioners. Such occasions will continue to provide hope in dealing with the long-term nature of the illness.

Information about treatment resources and health care professionals is certain to be shared. A family support organization may wish to keep its own list of accredited and knowledgeable practitioners. The American Anorexia Nervosa Association does this. The Canadian National Eating Disorder Information Centre supplies such information on request to support groups for the management of eating disorders, including information about waiting lists and accessibility. Articles with up-to-date information about treatment advances can be part of the organization's newsletter.

Some organizations sponsor annual conferences with speakers from various professions that treat aspects of eating disorders, such as Bulimia Anorexia Self-Help, Inc., in St. Louis, Missouri. Such conferences can reach health care professionals who want more knowledge and can provide information to family members. Other organizations sponsor coping-skills workshops, such as the Anorexia and Bulimia Parents' Support Group in Toronto.

Advocacy for Treatment, Research, and Prevention

Family members live with the pain caused by long waiting lists and overburdened treatment facilities. Those who feel that they are able to be public about their interest may wish to organize to lobby governmental and other funding sources, such as foundations and private corporations, to fund programs and information resources for the general public. Because family members and sufferers are directly affected, they can be effective voices.

Effects of Mutual Self-help Groups on Family Functioning

It has been widely assumed that family structure is changed or distorted by the presence of an eating disorder. Family life becomes overly concentrated on the sufferer and power struggles concerning eating, purging, and weight. The process of separation and individuation for the individual with an eating disorder may become severely compromised. Delayed or impaired launching of young adult children can profoundly affect the parental marital relationship. All family members' individual needs can be gradually neglected, and relationships with those outside the family tend to diminish, producing an intense sense of isolation.

Family groups can have a very beneficial effect on helping families make adaptive reactions to a chronic illness. Parents going together (or alone) to group meetings can identify positively with other parents. Independent parental activity will help to redraw intergenerational boundaries. Siblings can meet siblings from other families. When siblings choose not to attend, they may still feel permitted to resume their own lives when they see their parents begin to refocus on their own needs. Parents can advise other parents on how to allow the anorexic or bulimic individual to achieve appropriate separation without being abandoned. This need for both autonomy and support may be present even when the afflicted individual is living away from home. Adult patients will still benefit from feeling connected to the family, even while struggling with their own difficulties of independence.

Roles Professionals Can Play in Mutual Support Groups for Families

Since the beginning of the self-help movement, the role of health care professionals in mutual support groups has occasionally been a contentious issue. Some groups such as Alcoholics Anonymous and Recovery exclude health care professionals entirely except as affected participants. In other cases, family support groups are run in a clinical setting with health care professionals assuming most of the responsibilities.

There are many fundamental advantages to groups being led by non-professionals who are experiencing the problems of coping with an eating disorder at home on a daily basis. Such leaders provide participants with live models of surviving and coping. Such leadership is destigmatizing and illustrates the value of experiential (as opposed to "folk" or expert) knowledge. These leaders regularly facilitate the powerful positive effect of mutual understanding and support.

Health care professionals can fill many roles in facilitating the function of family support groups for the management of eating disorders. They can support the formation of a group by working with a core group of parents to publicize the first meetings. This is less complicated if a health care professional finds, for a core group, parents who are not his or her own clients. A health care professional with a broad array of skills and a keen awareness of community needs will be the most helpful in getting the first meetings under way. Agencies and hospitals can provide basic resources such as photocopying, meeting rooms, and information about where to seek incorporation and legal advice. Health care professionals play a pivotal role in informing the professional communities of the existence of the group. This is vital if referrals are to be made to the group. When the group decides to have information nights or to sponsor workshops, health care professionals can offer to speak or to help the group find speakers. When the group is well established, health care professionals can make a significant contribution by making ongoing referrals or serving on the board or committees. A successful group may find that its leaders are burning out after a few months or years of vigorous activity. The health care professional's skills may be helpful in enabling the leaders to find ways of bringing newer members into leadership roles and thus maintaining the group.

Within the actual support groups, health care professionals can facilitate and mediate the discussions by participants and be a symbol of support simply by being present. Despite the inevitable venting of frustration toward specific health care professionals and institutions, families of persons with eating disorders are extremely aware of the need for professional help for the afflicted family member. In this respect, they are very much in partnership with the health care professionals. One shared area of frustration will often be the long process of recovery.

At all times, health care professionals must be guided by respect for a group's autonomy and its right to self-determination. Health care professionals can derive much satisfaction from observing the development of empowerment in previously disempowered individuals. The role of the professional must be one of support and facilitation.

Summary

In this chapter, I have reviewed the nature of self-help mutual-aid groups in the context of multidimensional treatment for eating disorders. Family support groups are useful to their participants, because support groups are now available in most major health centers and many have continued to exist in a stable fashion, some now for much longer than a decade. The organizations appear to flourish particularly when there is a sense of ownership by the families of sufferers combined with a high degree of professional interest in and involvement with these organizations. Similarly, support groups function at their best when they are led by a partnership of seasoned parents and empathic, concerned health care professionals.

Many research questions occur. Longitudinal studies of the social and emotional functioning of the participants might clarify more concretely how the groups make a difference. The most helpful kinds and forms of information about the disorders need to be identified. There is a need for an empirical study of the effects of involvement in support groups on family and individual functioning. And there is a larger question: Is there a demonstrable positive effect either on successful outcome of treatment or on more successful adaptation to the disorder when individuals with eating disorders and their families are involved with mutual support groups?

Reference

Borkman T: Mutual self-help groups: strengthening the selectively insupportive personal and community networks of their members, in The Self-help Revolution. Edited by Gartner A, Reissman F. New York, Human Sciences Press, 1984

Index

Affective disorder, 53, 60
Alcohol addiction, 53, 60, 63, 100
All-American families, 52, 53
American Anorexia Nervosa
    Association, 145, 150
Anorexia and Bulimia Parents'
    Support Group, 150
Anorexia Bulimia Family Support
    Group, 145–146
Anorexia nervosa, 94, 103
    Maudsley Hospital study, 3–20
    multidimensional treatment,
        125–137
    relapse, 79
    See also Anorexia nervosa with
        bulimia nervosa; Early onset,
        long history anorexia nervosa;
        Early onset, short history
        anorexia nervosa; Late onset
        anorexia nervosa
Anorexia nervosa with bulimia
    nervosa, 104
    Maudsley Hospital study, 4, 6, 9,
        10, 12, 15, 16, 18
Appearance-consciousness, 52, 70,
    113, 115
Assessment. *See* Expressed emotion;
    Family assessment; Family
    Assessment Measure
Attachment and loss dynamics,
    54–57
Audiotape interviews, 7–8
Autonomy and separation, 113,
    114–115

Battle for initiative, 134–135
Battle for structure, 92, 130
Belief systems, 29, 37–38

Bulimia Anorexia Self-Help, Inc.,
    150
Bulimia nervosa
    attachment and loss dynamics,
        54–57
    family characteristics, 52–54, 70
    impasses in marital and family
        therapy, 74–79
    impasses in therapist-family
        metasystem, 71–74
    Maudsley Hospital study, 3–20
    medical dysfunctions, 60, 63, 69
    multidimensional treatment,
        125–137
    overprotective family, 98
    perfect family, 100
    relapse behavior, 79–81, 84
    "secret" bulimia, 91, 94–95, 100,
        133–134
    therapeutic issues, 58–60
    treatment problems, 60–64

Canadian Mental Health
    Association, 146
Canadian National Eating Disorder
    Information Centre, 146, 150
Center for Eating Disorders, 69
Chaotic family, 53, 98, 100
Communication styles, 113, 114
Confidentiality, 120
Conflict resolution
    bulimia nervosa, 52, 53, 54, 70,
        74, 77–78
    discharge planning, 136–137
    early onset, short history anorexia
        nervosa, 28, 29–30
    family relations group, 113, 114
Confrontations, 39, 42

155